Israel
vs.
America
vs.
the World

—

Hani Montan

Copyright © 2011 Hani Montan
All rights reserved.
Authored by Hani Montan
            Australia, NSW, Panania
Title: Israel vs. America vs. the World / Hani Montan
Edition: 1st ed.
Editor: Ted Gilley
Printed by CreateSpace
            7290 B. Investment Drive
            Charleston, SC 29418
            USA
ISBN-13): 9781456419578 (pbk.)
ISBN: 1456419579
Subjects: • International relations
             • Religion and politics
             • Israel—foreign relations
             • United States—foreign relations
Library of Congress LCCN: 2010918282
National Library of Australia (CIP)-Dewey Number: 327.5694
BISAC (category): Non-fiction
Author's earlier books: Thorny Opinion and Dads Gags
Paper colour: Off-white

Contents

Introduction

Money, nationalism, and religion are the destructive weapons deployed against human and international relations. These weapons are etched in the history of the rise and fall of empires. Currently, the American Empire, with its foreign policy controlled by Israel, is at centre stage and is the subject of this book.

America and Israel together, with their main ally, Britain, represent the axis of evil in the way they use their military power to conduct their relations with other countries, especially in the Islamic world.

America, Britain, and Israel don't understand that influence—not power—is ultimately the most valuable strategy. Influence comes from magnanimity and reaps greater gains. The use of power, on the other hand, results in resentment and counter-action, which ultimately weakens and destroys the aggressor. Military power was and will always be the driver behind the rise and fall of empires. History books are full of examples of far-reaching ambitions for world domination, especially during the reign of the Roman, the Ottoman, and the British empires. A brief description of the behaviour and the rise and fall of these three empires in Chapter 1 is presented only to refresh readers' memories and to help draw some parallels with the current single superpower, America.

The use of military power, the killings, and the destruction of infrastructures creates second-class nations and sects which have no hope left but to become militant.

The militancy and insurgency of the brutalised people are driven by their desire to survive, rather than to consider the adoption of a moderate ideology. The brutality of America and Israel doesn't leave the brutalised a chance to think of moderation. Using military and financial might, instead of applying wisdom and diplomacy in dealing with other people and countries is a recipe for disaster for both the conquered and the conqueror. America and Israel are ignoring the simple fact that injustice creates resentment and revolt—as demonstrated in their brutal actions in Palestine, Iraq, Lebanon, Pakistan, and Afghanistan.

Denying justice and inflicting extreme pain on their enemies (or their perceived enemies), America and Israel are sowing the seeds for revenge, not only in these oppressed countries, but throughout the Islamic world. Above all, America and Israel are operating on the "rather be feared than loved" principle, without taking into consideration that fear can either destroy people or drive them by triggering their survival instinct to fight.

Since winning the war in 1967 against the Arabs, Israel's politics have shifted to the far right, which caused the entrenchment of religious nationalism amongst its extremist far-right groups, especially the fanatical Jewish settlers. This has in turn encouraged America to shift its policy from an indirect control over Middle East oil to direct control through a military intervention. The architects of this shift in policy were some extremist Zionists, such as the Jewish Anti-Defamation-League and the Israeli lobby groups. These groups have the capacity to influence the American Congress, the American economy, and the media, including the election of any American president. The control of America's foreign policy by Israeli lobby groups is clearly demonstrated by America's war in Iraq. The false impression the Zionists and the Israeli lobby groups gave the American politicians about the convergence of Israel's and America's strategic interests was actually designed to benefit Israel at the expense of America. The war ended up creating chaos in Iraq and more enemies for America, especially throughout the Islamic world, which should be a cause for concern to all American citizens, because the war has accelerated the process of America's decline.

The Israelis don't seem to understand that the ultimate demise of America as a superpower will expose Israel to the world's anger and to direct Islamic revenge, especially from its 350 million Arab neighbours. The Israelis also don't seem to understand that the Americans may sooner or later come to the conclusion that Israel is a major liability to their country's national interests and decide to abandon it or even turn against it.

America and Israel should never ignore the simple lesson of history relating to the rise and fall of empires in which money, nationalism, and religion are generally combined to create the desire to expand by conquest without taking into consideration the conqueror's limited capacity and resources.

Readers are warned that in order to discredit this book, some extremist Zionists will vigorously attack it and tag it as anti-Semitic. This is their usual way of silencing the voices raised against the Israeli government's brutality in its quest to subjugate and destroy the powerless Palestinians.

The author is not and never will be anti-Semitic, as there are many moderate Jews around the world who are fighting for justice whom he admires. In fact, the majority of the sources referred to in this book are those of moderate and humanitarian Jews who were subjected to similar accusation by the same Jewish extremists. It should not escape the reader that the author admires the positive work of the prominent Israeli advocacy group Breaking The Silence, B'Tselem: the Israeli Information Centre for Human Rights in the Occupied Territories, and the genuine Israeli and American "peace now" movements that seek the establishment of a just and viable Palestinian state.

The author, however, is definitely against extremist Zionists, Christian Zionists, Muslim fundamentalists and all religious nationalists. These groups are the cause of all major conflict in the world. Their actions are leading the world into an environment similar to the one that culminated in the catastrophe of World War II.

The book focuses on the current state of world affairs and highlights the destructive role of Israel and America in human and international relations. It is my hope that the reader will find it informative and analytical.

The Author

Hani Montan is an Australian citizen, married with two daughters and one granddaughter.

In 1966, he was post graduated with a master of science degree in civil and industrial engineering.

In addition to extensive travel around the world, he has studied and worked in Iraq, Russia, and Algeria. To keep abreast of social, managerial, and technical developments, he has studied many subjects, which include project management, public relations, environmental protection, social and political science, formal logic, psychology, human relations, business administration and introduction to philosophy.

Montan worked at Sydney Water in the capacity of project engineer and group leader and also owned and managed a retail business.

The experience he has gained from working with people over many years, and his long interest in politics and social studies, have given him the motivation to write about many different subjects that might be useful to many readers, including this book.

This book is in total contrast with his earlier, humorous book titled *Dads Gags*, but is an extension of the thoughts expressed in his first book, *Thorny Opinion*, which dealt with social, political, religious, and environmental issues.

His blogs on various subjects can be found on *Open Forum.com.au* by googling Hani Montan.

Acknowledgements

It is not possible to write a complex book without reference to materials produced earlier by prominent writers, filmmakers, journalists, documentary makers, human right activists, philosophers, and freedom fighters. I would like to name and salute just few amongst many others of my heroes who were the main source of my knowledge and inspiration, especially in producing this book, which is dedicated to them and to our first granddaughter, **Raven**, who was born in January, 2011:

Julian Assange, founder of the website WikiLeaks. **Daniel Ellsberg**, a former US military analyst. **John Pilger**, a journalist and documentary maker. **Michael Moore**, an author, filmmaker, and political commentator. **Helen Thomas**, a journalist and author. **Robert Fisk**, a writer and journalist. **James Petras**, a retired professor of sociology. **John Mearsheimer**, an American professor of political science. **Paul Findley**, a Republican and a former member of the House of Representatives. **Sasha Polakow-Suransky**, an author and senior editor of *Foreign Affairs* magazine. **Michael Scheuer**, former CIA analyst. **Noam Chomsky**, an American philosopher, cognitive scientist, and political activist. **Bob Woodward**, an associate editor at the *Washington Post*. **James Cameron**, a filmmaker. **James Bamford**, a US intelligence expert. **Jimmy Carter**, former US president and author. **Norman G. Finkelstein**, an American historian. **Ilan Pappe**, a professor of social sciences and a historian. **Jacqueline Rose**, a British academic. **Grant F. Smith**, director of the Institute for Research of Middle Eastern Policy in Washington. **Christopher Hitchens**, an English-American author and journalist. **Alan Hart**, an author and former Middle East chief correspondent for Independent Television News. **Sara Dowse**, a novelist. **Thomas E. Ricks**, a Pulitzer Prize winner and former reporter for the *Wall Street Journal* and *Washington Post*. And for the many others I have unintentionally left out, I hope you forgive me.

Last but not least, I wish to extend my thanks to **Ted Gilley** for his excellent editing and formatting and to all the teams at CreateSpace for artwork, production, publication, and promotion of this book. Their diligence and professionalism are very much appreciated. It was a delightful experience dealing with so many nice and dedicated people. **Thank you all!**

Chapter 1

Rise & Fall of Empires

My intention in placing this subject at the beginning is for its relevance to the current international state of affairs and to highlight the problems facing America and its capacity to deal with the decline and the eventual demise of its Empire.

The brief history of the Roman, Ottoman, and British empires is provided to remind readers of the cyclical nature of the rise and fall of empires and to imagine the destiny of the world's single superpower, the American Empire.

Despite its military might, America is heading to a speedy decline. Its decline is directly related not only to its needs for market expansion and control of world's energy resources, but also to some of the extremist evangelicals and Zionist groups influencing its behaviour.

The most common elements in the rise and fall of empires were military power, market expansion, natio-nalism, and religion, which are the same forces driving America today, especially in the use of military might in its ambition to dominate the world and control its resources. Past conquests for expansion, spread of religion, exploitation of other nations, and grabbing their wealth boosted the feeling of superiority and nationalism of a conquering nation as a result of their economic gains at the expense of the conquered nations. Past empires' building conquests have always caused the impoverishment of the conquered nations, which left nothing for them but to revolt and to eventually destroy the conqueror and its empire.

Every famous historian has understood that all empires are "mortals." Yet every empire and every citizen of every empire insisted that their empire was the exception that could never be challenged and never fail. Unfortunately, America will soon discover that it is the next **"Mortal Empire."**

The Roman Empire

The territories controlled by ancient Rome through conquest or annexation between the 3rd century BC and the 3rd century AD stretched from north-western Europe to the Near East and encompassed all the lands of the Mediterranean. The formation of the Roman Empire began under the Roman Republic and by the end of the 1st century AD, the Roman Empire was already the greatest empire of the ancient world. However, at the end of the fifth century, economic decline and barbarian peoples' revolts on the frontiers of the empire led to the eventual collapse of its western front. The eastern front based in Istanbul was to continue, in one form or another, for many centuries, until its eventual fall to the Muslim Turks in 1453.

The control of an empire of this scale depended on a tightly controlled system of a strong and disciplined army. Provinces of the empire were controlled by Roman governors appointed by the emperor. The Roman army and a number of strategically placed forts ensured that the empire was defended against hostile local peoples, and an efficient network of roads was built both to allow troops to move swiftly within the empire and to facilitate trade. Tax revenues and valuable commodities such as grain, minerals, and slaves enriched Rome and financed its army. The many diverse peoples and cultures whose countries became part of the Roman Empire were, to varying degrees, united by Roman culture and Roman ideals of government and citizenship.

In essence, the empire had grown too big for its resources. Extended frontiers required a huge army— always a vast drain on revenues—and that in turn generated an increasingly unwieldy bureaucracy. Too many unproductive mouths were being fed by too few farmers and peasants. This situation was worsened in the areas most exposed to barbarian invasions, where conditions were most unstable. Political competition between rivals for power resulted in continual civil wars, which drained finances, depleted manpower, and exhausted the empire. Massive rates of inflation forced an increase of money supply to pay the army and administrators, reduced confidence in the currency, and inhibited economic production. Romans were caught in a cycle of economic depression and bureaucratic stagnation. All these factors were exacerbated by the ceaseless pressure on the frontiers of the empire and by the constant need for more troops and more taxes.

As Roman rule and Roman culture spread, so did Roman religion. The Romans applied a doctrine known as "Roman translation," under which native gods were seen as equivalent to, or as aspects of, the more familiar gods of Rome. This doctrine made the spread of Roman religion throughout the empire remarkably easy. At the same time, Roman society absorbed many religious trends from the provinces, which eventually included Christianity.

The Christian Church was behind all Roman institutions that finished up outliving the empire that produced it. It was the church, more than anything that was able to provide a measure of continuity after the collapse of physical power and civil administration. The papacy continued to be based in Rome and to exert enormous authority over most of Europe.

The Crusades against Muslims in the Middle East was for taking control of the Holy Land and were spearheaded by the Holy Roman Empire.

The Ottoman Empire

The Turkish Empire lasted from 1300 to 1922 and was centred on the region of modern Turkey. At its greatest extent it spanned three continents, covering the area from Hungary in the north to Aden in the south and from Algeria in the west to the Iranian frontier in the east. The Ottoman power also extended into the Ukraine and southern Russia.

Its name derives from its founder, the Turkish Muslim warrior "Osman," who established the dynasty which ruled over the empire throughout its history.

The rise of the Ottoman state was due to its attraction for waging a holy war (*jihad*) in the struggle against the Christian Byzantine Empire. Following the defeat and expulsion in 1338 of the Byzantines from Anatolia, the Turks began to extend their territories, and in 1354 they conquered Ankara in central Anatolia. In the same year they occupied Gallipoli on the European side of the strait of the Dardanelles, which became the base for their subsequent drive into south-eastern Europe. The greatest achievement was the 1453 conquest of Constantinople (Istanbul), which became the last capital city of the empire. By 1534, the empire extended vastly to include Syria, Iraq, Egypt, Algeria, Saudi Arabia, and other lands. These Islamic countries offered little resistance to the conquering Muslim Turks.

The Ottoman Empire was, in modern terms, multi-lingual, multi-ethnic, multicultural, and multi-religious. The majority of the population of the European provinces consisted of Christians of the Orthodox Church, some of whom had accepted Ottoman rule because it was less burdensome than Catholic domination. The old, pre-Ottoman Christian elites were either destroyed or assimilated in the Ottoman system and converted to Islam.

The Ottoman Empire reached the peak of its territorial extent in the sixteenth and seventeenth centuries when considerable gains were made in Iran and on the European front. Towards the end of the sixteenth century, however, the empire began to decline when the vast territories it occupied became impossible to control, especially when the revolt against the empire was spreading.

It is worth noting that the Ottoman Empire was in debt that rose from 17 percent of revenue in 1868 to 50 percent by 1877, which was one of other key reasons for its destruction.

Finally, the collapse and extinction of the Ottoman Empire was a result of World War I, when the government made the mistake of entering the war on the side of the Central Powers. The defeat of Germany meant the end for the Ottomans. The Ottomans suffered defeats at the hands of Russia in eastern Asia Minor, but in 1917–1918, when new British offensives began in Iraq and Syria, the Ottoman military forces were well in decline and by the time of the Armistice in October 1918, the Ottomans had lost everything but Anatolia. They lost not only the Arab provinces but suffered a partition of Anatolia.

In opposition to Allied plans, and in particular to the invasion of Smyrna by Greece in May 1919, an opposing Turkish nationalist movement had grown up under the leadership of Mustafa Kemal Ataturk, and this movement carried on armed resistance until, in 1922, the Greeks were defeated and driven out of Anatolia.

On November 1, 1922, the Ottoman dynasty was abolished and the empire came to an end. A year later it was replaced by the Republic of Turkey.

During its brutal existence, the Balkan states, especially Albania, Bosnia, the former Yugoslav republic of Macedonia, and Bulgaria were much oppressed and their progress was retarded, which was a cause of revolt. The civilisation of the Arab countries was stifled for many centuries and to date they have lost any potential for future advancement. In the beginning, to Muslims it was a matter of pride and comfort to be part of Islamic Ottomans—pride in its early victories, and comfort that it stood as a defence against the non-Muslim world. Later, however, especially in the nineteenth century when they started to interfere and control the lives of the people, Muslims and non-Muslims alike turned against them. This was the consequence of centralising the empire's power to ensure its survival, which needed a cumbersome army and government. There are similarities here to some of the reasons that led to the downfall of the Roman Empire.

The nationalistic and religious ideologies of Ottoman Islam and its political system, which lasted over 600 years, have retarded the civilisation of all countries under its control and caused the division between the Orthodox and Catholic churches in Europe.

The British Empire

The British Empire refers to a group of territories spread throughout the world, historically united by allegiance to the British crown, which at the peak of its expansion in the early twentieth century covered more than 20 percent of the earth. Essentially, it consisted of those territories that came under the formal jurisdiction of England from the late 1500s through the mid-twentieth century. The empire was controlled by a system of dependencies, colonies, and protectorates under the sovereignty of the British crown. Decentralisation by the granting of self-government to its dependencies and colonies was the best way to manage the vast territories under its control. This is in contrast to the centralised system used by the Ottoman Empire (and one of the reasons for its destruction).

Driven by its commercial ambitions and nationalism as well as its desire to compete with the French Empire in the seventeenth and eighteenth centuries, and aided by its maritime capacity, the United Kingdom was able to establish settlements and colonies in many part of the world, including America (lost in 1783), the Caribbean countries, Africa, India, China, Australia, and Canada. To maintain strong control of its vast colonies, it issued the Navigation Act of 1651, which established a closed economy between the empire and its colonies. The Navigation Act dictated that colonial exports and imports had to be shipped through the British market, with the British navy preventing other European powers from interfering with the Empire's trade.

Additionally, the Industrial Revolution began first in Great Britain, providing it a great wealth creation advantage as well as the advantage of an advanced banking and credit system. While the Ottoman Empire was in decline for a century after 1815, no single nation was able to make a bid for domination, allowing Britain to rise to its zenith in naval, colonial, and commercial terms based on its virtual monopoly of steam-driven industrial production. Industrialisation spread in the second half of the nineteenth century, tilting the balance of power, but also introduced more complicated and expensive weaponry that transformed the nature of war and made the world more vulnerable, less stable, and more complex.

During its peak, the British Empire established The Colonial Office and adopted suitable policies and management methods, including the establishment of high commissions for controlling its vast territories. But with its entry into World War I, Britain began to see the beginning of the end of empire. This decline culminated with its commitment to World War II and continued with declarations of independence by many of its colonies, starting with India in 1947.

It is worth noting that in 1931, the British Commonwealth, comprising mostly self-governing dependencies and other elements of the British Empire, was established as a symbolic acknowledgement of British sovereignty. It is also worth noting that the motto of British knighthood is "For God and the Empire," hoping that no future knights will be called "Knights of the Dead Empire."

Anyhow, the British were concerned with the cultural as well as political aspects of the empire, and religion played an important role in the development of modern imperialism. Their approach was part of the cultural intersection of war and religion, especially in the formation of the second British Empire. It is when the British became convinced that an empire of expanding trade is better than cultural, religious, and territorial control, and that the East, where it had a foot-hold (especially in India) is a better option for the expansion. This was after 1783 and following the loss of America as a result of the American War of Independence that culminated in the formation of the United States.

It is worth noting that after the United States became independent, it was no longer possible for Britain to send criminals into exile to North America. To continue the policy, a new destination was needed and the chosen destination was Botany Bay, Sydney, in what became known as New South Wales, Australia and later the whole continent of Australia was declared a British land. The aboriginal inhabitants were ignored as though they were animals and Australia was declared a "terra nullius," which means, belonging to no one. Like North America, this was a colony of settlement rather than merely of rule and exploitation, as in India and later in the Arab world. The British conquest in the East extended into Burma, Singapore, the Malayan peninsula, and Hong Kong.

All this was at a time when Britain's Protestant heritage came to the fore, as the nation defined itself through a series of wars against a hostile Catholic French. Religion was part of many smaller colonial conflicts of the era. Britain's imperial expansion came to be intimately linked with Protestant evangelism. Missionary groups grew enormously from the end of the eighteenth century, when they gained widespread currency in response to the conflicts of the Napoleonic era. By the 1850s, the idea of the Christian soldier defending the British Empire had emerged as a core element of national identity. This period was also the time of religious reform. The Anglican Church began to lose its close association with the British state and Catholicism gained increasing legitimacy, which heralded the gradual demise of the church. Religion played a key role in colonial expansion and in Britain's role as an imperial power. Generally speaking, religious nationalism always plays a major role in many forms of violence throughout the world.

Finally, because World War II had a massive impact on Britain's resources, the British Empire came to an end. It was estimated that one-quarter of national wealth was lost and the national debt tripled, reaching the equivalent of about one-third of gross domestic product. Britain was living beyond its means before and during the war and was financed by foreign countries, chiefly America. The debt incurred as a result of World War II brought the British Empire to its knees and heralded the start of the American Empire.

From 1949, the British Empire became the Commonwealth of Nations, as former British dependencies obtained sovereignty but retained ties to the United Kingdom.

The American Empire

Following the demise of the British and French empires as a consequence of World War II, America has emerged not only as a superpower but as the newest empire. To date it has no rival, especially since the collapse of the Soviet

Union. Lending money to a post-World War II devastated Europe and establishing a foothold in the Middle East to control the energy resources was the foundation stone of the American Empire. This was at the expense of the French and the British who had become heavily indebted and whose power had drastically diminished. The financial and military power, the benefit of the brain-drain following World War II, especially the highly educated and motivated Jewish and other European immigrants, coupled with its own embrace of technical education, placed America on a growth path that drove it to evolve into an imperialistic power. The fast growth and industrialisation required new markets and control of energy sources, especially when the country started to live beyond its means.

Following the end of the Cold War, however, and on becoming an undisputed single superpower, America chose to adopt an extremist aggressive approach to international relations. Behind its aggression is the alliance between the extreme evangelical religious right groups and the neo-conservative hawks (some extremist Zionists and the Israel lobby groups). These groups favour the Republican Party to govern, not only because of its nonsecular attitude and total commitment to Israel, but for its adoption of an extreme capitalist platform. These groups were able to convince the Americans of America's exceptionalism and that America is indispensable; and that its national interest had no limit—a claim that has been proven to be totally misleading and false.

Embarking on simultaneous unnecessary wars in Iraq, Afghanistan and covert war in Pakistan has stamped it as an aggressive imperialistic power that is provoking Islamic militancy and placed it on a path of steep decline. The life of an aggressive imperialistic power that lacks the diplomatic skills and ability to conquer the heart of people is destined to be short. America, before considering its weakness, is challenging the world and creating a huge backlash, which is proving to be beyond its ability to control, no matter how many rockets it is able to fire.

In its endeavour to control the world, America is provoking major resentment and resistance, which will culminate in its defeat; a much worse defeat than it suffered in Vietnam, because the current war has religious overtone aimed against 1.5 billion Muslims.

In their book *Unintended Consequences: The United States at War,* professors Kenneth J. Hagan and Ian J. Bickerton demonstrate that America often embarks on unnecessary wars without proper analysis and often with total ignorance of local conditions. The authors detail America's wars from the War of Independence to the war in Iraq. The raging war in Afghanistan is the one that will produce probably the highest level of unintended consequences, that is, of engulfing the region in a nuclear fight between India and Pakistan or at least the collapse of Pakistan and the triumph of Muslim fundamentalists in both Afghanistan and Pakistan. No matter what, Pakistan's nuclear arsenal will be extremely difficult to manage and could lead to an unpredictable catastrophic outcome. (See Chapter 5.)

The unintended consequences of the war in Iraq are the ethnic and sectarian fighting and the strengthening of Iran's influence in the region, especially in defense of its nuclear program. This is in addition to exposing millions of Christian citizens in Islamic countries to genocide as a consequence of the religious nationalistic clash between the extremist Zionists and Christian Zionists on the one hand and the Arabs and the Islamic world on the other. America's and Israel's aggression against Islamic countries is making Christians an easy target for Islamic insurgency and revenge. The killing of Christians and the attacks on their churches have already started, and nothing will stop it. Over the past seven years, Iraqi Christians have been the target of violence, including murder and abductions. Hundreds of Iraqi Christians have been killed and several churches have been attacked since the US-led invasion to oust Saddam Hussein in 2003. These killings and attacks on churches are now spreading throughout the Islamic world. The recent attacks by Al-Qaeda on Coptic churches in Egypt, where eight millions Coptic Christians live, could develop into civil war.

Hagan and Bickerton have correctly concluded that the unintended consequences of America's wars were far worse than their originally desired benefits and that this has resulted in catastrophic foreign policy. The miscalculation of consequences has been reflected in the continuation of America's involvement in the defeated country's chaotic mess for many years after the war at a major cost and a negative impact on its national security.

Worse still, America's foreign policy is influenced by the Zionist movement to the benefit of Israel with little regard to America's national interests. Furthermore, the

Zionists' influence is reflected on America's domestic and economic policies through the Israel lobby groups' control of Congress.

The advocated theory of extremist Zionists is unilateral and assertive war, seen as essential in achieving benevolent world hegemony and in shaping the international environment to the advantage of the United States. Unfortunately, the theory has a built-in dangerous unintended consequence and a miscalculation of the lesson of history; specifically, the rise of Third Reich and World War II. Creating a war machine to conquer the world is fraught with danger. It embodies the rise of nationalism, which develops into fascism and a government becoming very secretive by virtue of being controlled by its military elites, which gradually take the country into the path of a dictatorship. America, as it stands, is a secretive and arrogant country, as can be seen from the WikiLeaks documents and the State Department's diplomatic cables that were released in December 2010.

Moderate Jews should be vigilant against the zeal of some of their extremist Zionist leaders who place too much emphasis on short-term gains while ignoring the ultimate consequences, especially regarding America's decline and eventual demise. One of the main dangers for Israel stems from the linking of its strategic interests with those of America, without taking into consideration the fact that America, for its own strategic interests, is using Israel to spearhead control over the fragmented oil-rich Arab countries and to cement its presence in the Middle East. Israel, in turn, is using America in its short-term quest to expand and colonise Palestine, but when America becomes comfortable with its control of the Middle East, it will need stability. Israel will then become a major liability for its provocative actions against the Palestinians and its Arab neighbours.

To achieve their common short-term objectives in the Middle East, America and Israel came to the conclusion that Arab nationalism is the major stumbling block in the way of meeting their objectives and therefore must be destroyed. In the process, they overlooked the fact that Arab nationalism is directly related to the Islamic religion, hence the war on Arabs is perceived as a war on Islam dressed up as a war on terrorism. It is in fact a religious, nationalistic war that nobody can win and its ultimate unintended consequence will be "assured mutual destruction."

The demise of the American Empire will not only be caused by its foreign policy, but also by its social, political, and economic structure. Based on current trends, its debt could reach 300 percent of GDP by 2050 from 10 percent of GDP in 2010. This and other detailed analyses can be seen in book entitled *The Ascent of Money: The Financial History of the World* by the prominent British historian and Harvard Business School professor Niall Ferguson. In it he write, "The fall of empires in history occurs for many reasons but there is one thread through most falls, which is overextending the empire's commitment past its ability to resource. Most empires fell because the desired-expected-anticipated return on the investment of expansion failed to materialise. Rome fell because it failed to bring all its conquered territories into its hegemony; the territories always retained their sense of tribal/racial identity and regarded the Romans as overlords. The British Empire decayed (rather than fell) because it lacked the will and resources to continue after the Second World War but its core remained untouched. The US will probably go the same way unless its creditors determine that destruction of the economy is a more commercially beneficial outcome than allowing it to decay."

America's unsustainable public debt, incurred largely to finance its unnecessary wars. Reduction of its debt is hindered by partisan political structure, which could bring it to the brink of total default. In the meantime, it will keep printing money until hyper-inflation catches up with it. This is when the reality will hit the Americans, prompting a socio-political revolution that will herald the end of the fifty-years-young empire. Its ultimate demise will come from the religious war that is being waged against Islam and in its continuing support of Israel's aggression against the Palestinians and their Arab neighbours.

Chapter 2

Socio-political Cause of America's Decline

In his book *Rise and Fall of the Great Powers*, the British historian Paul Kennedy demonstrates how over the past 500 years nations that became great powers declined as their growth rate slowed and their spending on defence continued to increase. The decline can be eased or worsened by smart (or stupid) policy decisions. He provides convincing evidence that the theory of "wars are won by economic might and not because providence is on the side of the good guys. All empires are mortal, and can kill themselves by economic over-extension." Kennedy predicts that American deficit spending will become a major problem in the future.

Living beyond its means and its wars in Iraq, Afghanistan and covert war in Pakistan are the main causes of its entrenched budget deficit, which is expanding. America is deluding itself in thinking that its gradual withdrawal of troops from Iraq to a surge in Afghanistan will bear fruit. America has sown the seeds in Iraq and is doing the same in Afghanistan and Pakistan that will culminate in a civil war in these countries. The civil war will especially engulf the nuclear state Pakistan, which will have major consequences for the world. All that America is doing is establishing, training, and equipping loyal corrupt groups that may become capable of fighting the militants for their own self-preservation, hoping that in the process they will destroy each other. It is wishful thinking because sooner or later, Iraq, Afghanistan, and Pakistan will become failed states like Somalia, Congo, Ivory Coast, Algeria, Libya, Tunisia, Morocco, Egypt, Jordan, Lebanon, Sudan, Nigeria, and Yemen, which will be of no benefit to America other than a huge cost to its national interest and security, as these countries are increasingly becoming a major source of ever-increasing terrorism.

At the urging of the Israeli government, America may decide to add Iran and Syria to the list of failed states. The questions to be asked: How will these failed states be of any benefit to the world? Isn't it obvious that most of these countries are Islamic? Isn't most of the world's oil owned by Islamic states? What are the consequences of these wars? America will not be exempt from the laws of history. The world's history is rich with examples of economic over-extension and repeated military conflicts that only result in weakening a country's economic base, leading to its demise.

In my earlier book, *Thorny Opinion,* I came to the conclusion that the ambition of a highly developed and industrialised country to expand beyond its borders is following the same pattern of the rise and fall of earlier empires. America's use of its military power for economic expansion and the control of world's resources is history repeating itself and is proof that when humans are corrupted by greed and power they become blinded, develop short memories, and become incapable of learning from the lessons of history.

Earlier wars that culminated in World War II resulted in eclipsing France and irretrievably weakening Britain, brought defeat to the Axis nations, and left a bipolar world with military and economic resources roughly in balance. World War II started when Germany met the criteria of combining the three elements for war: the need for market expansion outside its territory, nationalism, and religion. (Hitler's Catholic beliefs were confusing, as he often referred to providence and God and the ritualistic pageantry of Nazism and tagged Christ as a "fighter." Although, his beliefs bordered on paganism and contradicted Christian teachings, the German Catholic Centre was fully behind him, especially after receiving official recognition from Pope Pius XI.)

America now is in an advanced stage of meeting the same criteria. It is engaged in three minor wars in Iraq, Afghanistan and covert war in Pakistan with a possible fourth, much bigger war, in Iran. All these wars have the potential to become an all-out war against Islam.

America is spending more on warfare than it is getting back from its attempt to dominate the world. In the process, it has accumulated debt of over $14 trillion (as at January 2011), which will take many years to pay off. The debt is mainly the result of its aggressive approach to international relations, which is driven by extremist

Zionists and Christian Zionists. These groups are in the minority but they are so vocal and powerful that they have the capacity to corrupt American democracy. They have converted American democracy to run by the power of money and their narrow extremist ideology. The Israel lobby groups alone have the capacity to unseat any congressman who dares to go against their interests. They do so by withdrawing financial support and financing an alternative candidate who is willing to toe their line.

The corruption of America's democracy can also be observed in its government's secrecy and in its reaction to WikiLeaks' publication in December 2010 of the State Department's diplomatic cables, which exposed its arrogant foreign relations. Its reaction to the scandal was to "shoot the messenger" by targeting Julian Assange and treating him as an enemy of the state. All the signs are pointing to America being hijacked by the far-right elements that are always ready to silence the voice of reason.

Political Polarisation

The political polarisation of the Republican and Democrat parties is gradually leading America to self-destruction. Earlier, Congress operated more on a conscience vote basis, but now is operating more strictly on a party loyalty basis, which is similar to the Westminster system, in which seldom does a parliamentarian crosses the floor to vote against the party line. Toeing the party line by the Republicans is now matched by the Democrats, hence the polarisation. There is no logic, for example, when one party has the capacity to veto tax rises, whilst the other party has the capacity to veto spending cuts. One of them must be wrong. The previous capacity of Congress to hear the voices of minorities is now lost. The move to party authoritarianism usually results in placing the power in the hands of few influential members of the party, which makes a mockery out of any democracy.

The disadvantage to the country was highlighted on August 2, 2010, when Sarah Palin, who is the symbol of polarisation in America, urged Barack Obama to play the "war card" when America was in desperate need of just the opposite. She wanted the US attorney general sacked for his handling of terrorism cases, and accused the president of being too relaxed about national security by saying that Barack Obama would not be re-elected unless he plays the war card and declares war on Iran or does whatever he can to support Israel. She also said, "America needs a commander in chief and not an attorney." Playing the "war card" is the essence of the American political far-right psyche and on which they structure their economy and their relationship with rest of the world. This is why America has over 750 military bases around the world, posing threats to many countries and creating insurgencies.

Partisan politics places the interest of one political party and its ideology above the interest of the country, especially when one party is determined to defeat the other party at any cost. The polarisation between the Republicans and the Democrats and the constant use of the filibuster rule in the Senate to obstruct legislation, even when it is in America's national interest, impedes

America's progress. The constitutional rules of filibuster were originally designed for the purpose of debating to reach a better outcome for the country; it is now having the opposite effect. Unfortunately, the ideology-driven interest of one party is becoming more important than the country. Since Barack Obama's historic victory, hope has given way to fear fuelled by the far-right media, which created a new class of disappointed and angry Americans who want to bring the establishment down to safeguard their liberty. The Republican Party is being driven by the extremist Tea Party under the political slogan, "We're taking back the country from the socialist." This is having a major impact on political polarisation in America; it is reflected in Congress by making the passage of legislation on a bipartisan basis extremely difficult. America now is a country in a state of psychological depression and economic stagnation when a bipartisan approach is the only way out—but unfortunately, its corrupted democracy is hindering it from moving forward.

The other disadvantage to the country is caused by the vocal media barons and the religious nationalists and evangelicals, and the Israel lobby groups, which have major political influence in controlling the Republican Party. The power of these groups, bolstered by their great financial resources, is shown in their capacity to dictate election results by propaganda and by financing candidates of their choosing to unseat any "disobedient" congressman. American democracy is driven by the power of money, media, and religion.

The political polarisation is happening at a time when maximum national unity is needed to restore its strength. America's decline is being accelerated by its huge budget deficit while it wages unwinnable wars around the world.

America's political polarisation is also a reflection of the social divide between the rich and the poor. The rich are becoming richer and the poor are left behind, which sooner or later will become an additional threat to a fragile democracy. However, the immediate threat to America's democracy is emanating from the Israel lobby groups, which place Israel's national interests ahead of America's and from the extreme evangelicals, who place God ahead of the country.

During the 2008 presidential election campaign, Senator Joe Lieberman readily switched allegiance from the Democrats to become independent, or more to the point, pro-Republican, in his hope that the Republicans would be more inclined to declare war on Iran than the Democrats would. He became a major supporter of the Republican presidential candidate John McCain, who at the time was advocating a war on Iran. The impression Mr. Lieberman has conveyed is that his priority is the protection of Israel, no matter what, and how much it will cost America. Accordingly, it could be construed that an unfortunate America is saddled with influential people whose loyalty appears to belong elsewhere.

Finally, political polarisation is further aggravated by the Supreme Court's ruling on political campaign finances, handed down in March 2010. The ruling allows corporations to act as "individuals," which lets them donate anonymously to parties or candidates. It has the potential to encourage huge corporations to sponsor legislation directly or indirectly. It is a tragic decision for America that is based on freedom of speech and the First Amendment, but in this case it will entrench the influence of money on election results. It is the single biggest political decision by the Supreme Court that has huge implications on all future elections' outcomes. It has the potential to further poison the political atmosphere by entrenching the role of money in elections that are driven by propaganda, distortion of facts, and the art of deception. This ruling will make a total mockery of American democracy. Corporations are now able to bankroll candidates, especially in paying for the advertising of candidates who are willing to sponsor legislation that is to their advantage. Payment for costly advertising is not considered a donation under the law; therefore it isn't subject to disclosure.

This proved to be a bonanza for vested interests during the mid-term elections in November 2010, when the total spending exceeded $4 billion and when the media became saturated with negative and facts-distorting advertising, the outcome of which was the delivery of a divided government at a time when the country needed unity.

It is unthinkable that freedom of speech can apply to a money machine that controls and owns the whole system. It must be a sad day for American democracy when a right-wing organisation such as Fox News can openly sponsor and promote extreme religious-right Republican politicians and at the same time degrade Democrats. This could be the outcome of stacking the Supreme

Court with right-wing judges during the George W. Bush administration.

Racism and Discrimination

Racism and discrimination in America are alive and well. Historically, the country has been dominated by white people and the rest were treated as second-class citizens. Prejudice and racism is often directed toward Native Americans, African Americans, Muslim Americans, Asian Americans, Mexican Americans, Hispanic Americans, illegal immigrants, and other minority groups.

It is estimated that there are 11 million badly exploited illegal immigrants in America who have no legal or social protection. During economic growth, illegal immigrants, especially Mexicans, are allowed in the country to work for low wages, but they are hounded or deported during economic slow-downs. Illegal immigrants, whose cheap labour has for many decades helped build American economic growth, are now being demonised.

Racial discrimination has occurred in employment, housing, education, and by government. American legislators had earlier recognised that people come to America for either money or freedom. Accordingly, they decided to end the formal racial discrimination, which was officially banned in the mid-twentieth century. Since then, racial discrimination has become socially unacceptable, except in racial politics, where it remains a major problem, especially in racist attitudes and prejudice against African Americans, illegal immigrants, Hispanics, and Muslims.

The recent immigration laws introduced in Arizona that are aimed at cracking down on illegal immigrants is a good example of how prejudiced America is. The laws that allow police to check a person's immigration status, which compels the immigrants to carry their papers at all times, will lead to racial profiling. Although Arizona judge Susan Bolton issued a temporary injunction to block some part of the laws, the matter will be subject to appeal and may end up in the Supreme Court.

This blatant discrimination is in addition to the discrimination against all economically disadvantaged groups who are left behind by America's extreme capitalism. The eventual revolt and uprising of these groups will add to the causes that are driving America's decline.

Leaving behind the black people in New Orleans at the height of Hurricane Katrina, when 80 percent of the city was flooded, is a good example of America's racism. In a shameful lack of action and neglect by the Bush administration, thousands of mostly black and poor citizens were abandoned. Additionally, more African Americans suffered the brutality of the white vigilantes and the police by killings and the official cover-up of racially motivated violence. The armed white militias cordoned off many of the streets and posted signs that boasted, "We shoot looters." Many people were killed and later several police officers and white civilians were indicted. The Justice Department has started investigations into civil rights violations. What happened in New Orleans displayed a systemic contempt and the dormant racism of white Americans against black Americans.

The fragility of race relations in America can also be observed in the case of Shirley Sherrod, a black public servant who was sacked in July, 2010, as the Department of Agriculture's director of rural development in Georgia after a conservative website accused her of making racists remarks which were captured on a video it posted online. The two and a half minute clip, taken from a forty-three-minute speech that Ms. Sherrod gave in March 2010 immediately drew the attention of the White House and department officials who feared an attack from extreme-right commentators on the Fox News channel. She was sacked before it was known that the clip was only a small part of her speech, which when it was shown out of context conveyed a negative message. The fact was, the speech actually conveyed a positive race relations message. Taking Ms. Sherrod's words out of context was originated by a right-wing website called "BigGovernment.com." Fox News, being a far-right wing media organisation that never misses an opportunity to turn a racial positive into a negative, headlined the story "Racism Caught on Tape." This resulted in the sacking of a black person with a genuine purpose of promoting harmonious race relations in an America that is poisoned by entrenched racial prejudice.

Although her sacking was followed by many apologies, including one from the president, the episode highlighted how uneasy race relations in America are and how the administration of America's first black President was extremely sensitive to any charge or accusation against him that he may be tolerating the so-called "black racism" at a time when the blacks are fighting against white racism.

Discrimination, on the other hand, can be illustrated by the reaction to the proposal to build a mosque and Islamic community center two blocks away from New York's Ground Zero called the "Cordoba Initiative." The objection of the extreme right groups against the location of the center came despite the fact that two other mosques that have existed for decades are within four and twelve blocks, respectively, of Ground Zero.

The following are samples of stands taken by some public figures, groups, and organisations against the Islamic center:

- The American Centre for Law and Justice, a conservative advocacy group founded by the evangelical minister Pat Robertson, announced it would challenge the New York City regulation panel's decision in a state court.
- The proposed mosque has emerged as a national political issue, with prominent members of the Republican Party such as former vice presidential candidate Sarah Palin and the former House of Representatives Speaker Newt Gingrich voicing their opposition. Gingrich has labeled those behind the project radical Islamists and compared them to Nazis. "Nazis don't have the right to put up a sign next to the Holocaust Museum in Washington," he said.
- Pamela Geller, executive director of the Stop Islamisation of America activist group said, "What could be more insulting and humiliating than a monster mosque in the shadow of the World Trade Center buildings that were brought down by an

Islamic jihad attack? Any decent American, Muslim or otherwise, wouldn't dream of such an insult."

- The Jewish Anti-Defamation League has come out against the planned mosque and Islamic community centre near Ground Zero, saying "the location is counterproductive to the healing process of 9/11." And further the ADL said, "The group behind the plan, the Cordoba Initiative, has the legal right to build at the site, but some legitimate questions have been raised about funding and possible ties with groups whose ideologies stand in contradiction to our shared values. Ultimately this is not a question of rights, but a question of what is right." And further, the ADL said, "In our judgment, building an Islamic centre in the shadow of the World Trade Center will cause some victims more pain—unnecessarily— and that is not right."

- Following his endorsement of the plan, President Obama was stung by criticism from Republicans who described the plan as an affront to the families of victims of the September 11 attacks. In reply, Obama said, "I am not endorsing the plan, but simply speaking in support of the broad principle that in America we treat everybody equally and in accordance with the law, regardless of race, regardless of religion. I was not commenting, and I will not comment, on the wisdom of making the decision to put a mosque there." It was ridiculously unfortunate to see the US president back-pedaling by denying his endorsement of the plan out of fear of a backlash, as opinion polls put public opposition to the Islamic centre as high as 70 percent. The president's reversal displayed a lack of leadership. This is when the nation was in a state of anxiety and leadership was in desperate demand, especially when the Republicans were fuelling public opinion in playing the poisonous religious and race-relations cards ahead of November 2010, mid-term congressional elections. Judging by the statements of the Jewish lobby groups, Sarah Palin, and Newt Gingrich, it appears that the Republicans and their sponsors have no hesitation about turning Americans against each other in their fight for the control of Congress.

- During the proposed Islamic centre controversy, the extremist evangelical pastor Terry Jones, who heads the Dove World Outreach Center in Gainesville, Florida, vowed to burn the Koran on the ninth anniversary of September 11. His idea was to send a message to Muslim radicals by saying, "Instead of us being blamed for what other people will do or might do, why don't we send a warning to them? Why don't we send a warning to radical Islam and say, don't do it. If you attack us, we will attack you." He further said, "The Koran torching [is] aimed to remember those who were brutally murdered on September 11 and to send a warning to the radical element of Islam."

So the pastor wanted to burn the Koran as a warning to radical Muslims without taking into consideration, first, that the act of burning the Koran is an extremely radical act which only highlights the existence of extremism on both sides. Second, the move could trigger outrage around the Islamic world, as well as stoke a growing anti-Muslim tide of feeling in America. Third, such a stupid act and the consequential angry backlash can endanger the lives of many American troops and civilians serving in the Islamic world. The question should be asked: Is this another proof that religious fanatics usually place God ahead of their country? Are Islamophobic Christian and Jewish fanatics provoking all moderate Muslims into becoming radicals? Although the pastor has abandoned his plan to burn 200 copies of the Koran, the damage he caused in stirring up religious hatred was enormous. His destructive act has provoked worldwide condemnation and huge backlash throughout the Islamic world.

As can be seen, bigotry and religious venom is a reflection of Americans' intolerance towards Muslims. Some extremist Americans are changing the war from a war against terrorism to a war against Islam. This is being fuelled by extremist politicians and a biased media at a time when moderate Muslims, under the Cordoba Initiative, aim is to improve relations between Islam and the West by hosting leadership conferences for young American Muslims and organising programs on Arab-Jewish relations, building civil society in the Muslim world, empowering Muslim women, and steering the world back to a course of mutual recognition and respect.

The irony is that the head of the Cordoba Initiative is Imam Feisal Abdul Rauf, who is a practitioner of the Sufi strain of Islam—the most moderate and peaceful form of the religion. This imam has written for the *Washington Post* and has been consulted by the FBI and the State Department to help them to explain to Muslims around the world what America is about. He has devoted all his life to peacemaking and believes that the real enemy out to destroy Islam is Al-Qaeda. In return, his project received the most poisonous bigotry from the extremist Christians and Jews.

The heated debate across America over the construction of an Islamic centre two blocks from Ground Zero is still reverberating in all Islamic countries and across the world. The bitter division it has created in America has become a symbol of America's shocking relations with the Muslim world; Muslims viewed the rejection of the mosque as a rejection of Islam. The demonisation of Islamic religion is a dangerous political ideology. It is dangerous when they connect all Muslims to September 11 and connect terrorism and extremism to Islam. This is discrimination at its worst and it is driven by some religious nationalists who have the idea that America should lead the world under the banner of Jesus. They have identified Islam as their enemy that must be defeated. This attitude unfortunately is creating a violent reaction; Osama bin Laden is one of its by-products. The aggressive attitude of some extremist Christians and Jews towards Islam is now perceived as the "new Crusades," which in the opinion of extremist Muslims requires mobilisation for jihad against the infidels. It must be emphasised again that a religious war against 1.5 billion Muslims cannot be won. To secure the world's future, it is essential to curb extremism on all sides before it is too late; it is the duty of all moderates around the globe to act now, as they are the people best equipped to control the extremists within.

Using the construction of an Islamic centre as pretext to attack Muslims is an act of aggression, especially when considering that the people who died on 9/11 represented a broad spectrum of religious persuasions, including American Catholics, Protestants, and Jews, atheists, and American Muslims. Promoting the idea that Islam is bad, is very provocative and doesn't take into consideration that *all* religions are bad. Every religious group and sect considers the scripture of their holy book the only truth and that all others' holy books are wrong, including different interpretations of their own scripture.

Discrimination and bigotry expose America's split personality in its constitutional and cultural aspects, which means that the First Amendment of the US Constitution has lost its meaning. Dealing with all Muslims as if they are cut from the same cloth is very unfair for the simple reason that millions of American Muslims are loyal citizens and cherish America. Equating all Muslims as enemies and denying them the right to build a mosque, regardless of their having had nothing to do with the September 11 attack is in total conflict with the American Constitution. It is more so when such a moderate Muslim organisation that has planned the Islamic centre and has passed through all legal rules and regulations required by New York City has been subjected to humiliation and rejection by extremist religious groups of Christian Zionists and extremist Zionists and their political leaders.

The questions to be asked: If the same site were owned and developed as a Christian or a Jewish centre, would the reaction be the same? Do these extremist Christians and Jews realise that their attitude is provoking an equally extreme reaction? Do these extremists realise that maginalising any group in society provokes resentment and revolt? Why are extremist Christians and Jews using September 11 to marginalise all Muslims by painting them with the same brush? Why do these extremists think that the First Amendment, which protects freedom of religion, is meant only for them and not for others? Who will benefit from destroying America as a religiously, ethnically, and racially tolerant country? Who will benefit from living in such a fragmented society?

Discrimination and bigotry against American Muslims is only a small part of the total picture of America's aggression against Islamic countries, which is demonstrated in its policies of torturing Muslim prisoners, unconditional support for Israel, the invasion of Iraq and Afghanistan, and the killing of many innocent Muslim civilians. **Please wake up!**

The Tea Party Movement and the Republican Party

The Tea Party is a loosely organised movement of extreme right-wing political groups and individuals. An extremely conservative wing of the Republican Party, its ideology is based on a form of capitalism that favours the rich. It motivates its followers with slogans such as "Constitutionally limited government supports maximum individual liberty." Their behaviour however, indicates that the liberty they are after is for the rights and the extreme-rights, but not for anyone else.

The movement doesn't have a formal structure, which makes it attractive to many rogue activists, racists, and religious fundamentalists. It advocates a voluntary (non-governmental) social security and health insurance system as a way of achieving smaller government and lower taxes. Its strategy to gain governing power is to frustrate and seize the wheels of the more progressive Democrats and then to complain that their opponents are achieving nothing. It is founded as a parody of the original "Boston Tea Party," which was formed in 1773 by a group of colonists dressed up as Indians, who, to protest high taxes, boarded a British ship and threw tea in Boston harbour rather than paying taxes on it.

The current group is formed to protest against its own party, which it views as not being extreme or conservative enough. Their aim is to defeat the Democrats at any cost; they target individual Democrats with intimidation and threats as well as purging the less conservative Republicans. The forming of such a group is a good indication of the mood of extreme-rights Americans towards nationalism, religious aggression, and racism. It has the potential to become anti-Semitic, as its emergence is similar in concept to the rise of fascism and Nazism before World War II. This movement could develop into an aggressive power capable of curtailing the influence of the American Zionists on America's financial system, its foreign policy, and its social fabric. This is despite the fact that some of its current leaders are allied with some of the extremist Zionists in their undeclared war against Islam.

The Tea Party movement is a symptom of the decay of America's political system and will contribute to its ultimate disintegration. The rise of extreme right-wing ideology is part of the nervous tension and an indication of America's social and economic decline. The group is creating a dangerous division within America's politics and society in general. It has been suggested that the intense rhetoric that has characterised the Tea Party movement's approach to political debate could have played a part in inciting the attack on congresswoman Gabrielle Giffords by Jared Lee Loughner on January 2, 2011. Some of the fiercest recent comments and metaphors of armed insurrection have been associated with the grassroots Tea Party movement. Secretary of State Hillary Clinton said, "This shooting is an example of why people should reject radical ideologies."

Extremism is promoted by the likes of radio talk show host Rush Limbaugh, with his inflammatory comments against all moderate politicians. The popularity and power of Limbaugh, who has the biggest radio talk show audience in America and whom no Republican politician dares to contradict, is an indication of the entrenchment of racism and religious bigotry in the American social fabric. Limbaugh makes outrageous claims with impunity, as can be seen in some of his statements, for example, "Obama and Oprah are only successful because they are black." He calls Obama a "halfrican American" who is not black but Arab because Obama's father was from Kenya. (Arabs comprise less than one percent of Kenya's population.) This is an example of an attempt to degrade the president of the United States on racial grounds, despite the fact that Obama graduated from Harvard Law School.

In another statement, Limbaugh said, "Have you ever noticed how all composite pictures of wanted criminals resemble Jesse Jackson?" The highlight of his statements, however, is when he said, "I mean, let's face it, we didn't have slavery in this country for over a hundred years because it was a bad thing. Quite the opposite: slavery built the South. I'm not saying we should bring it back; I'm just saying it had its merits. For one thing, the streets were safer after dark."

Since the majority of Americans have become more accepting of blacks, Limbaugh has decided to play against its new racial fears. He has managed to make religious and racist attacks against four of the most admired and respected people in the past one hundred years: Martin Luther King Jr., Nelson Mandela, Colin Powell, and Barack Obama.

Limbaugh also mocked the Chinese president, Hu Jintao, during Hu's visit to the US in January 2011. Limbaugh lampooned Hu's manner of speaking by childishly repeating the words "ching chong, ching chong, chong." In doing so, he ridiculed one of the world's oldest languages, insulted the Chinese American and Asian American communities, and above all, he attempted to insult an intelligent and respected man.

This is the Republican Party today. Limbaugh's racist statements are echoed by Sarah Palin's supporters at her rallies. Sarah Palin is now leading the charge against every Republican congressman who is considered not conservative enough. Her endorsement of Christine O'Donnell as a candidate for the November 2010 mid-term senate elections is a clear indication of the direction these extremists are taking. Ms, O'Donnell is known for her Christian fundamentalism, whom with Palin's support has stood and won the race against Mike Castle who was the officially endorsed Republican candidate. This episode is an ugly example of what America has in store. Luckily, Ms. O'Donnell didn't win the seat. It is however, fanatics like her and Sarah Palin who have the capacity to sweep the nation along with them in a momentum of euphoric religious nationalism that could be hard to counter. Their success in influencing the results of the mid-term elections by helping the Republicans take control of the House of Representatives will have major implication for America's political and economic stability. It will also make the rest of the world wary of a major shift in America's foreign policies—especially in relation to the Middle East—when the pro-war Republicans take total control of Congress and the White House.

It is ironic that the Republicans' winning control of the House of Representatives and nearly the Senate in the mid-term elections was the result of a backlash against the economic stagnation and high unemployment which they themselves caused during the presidency of George W. Bush. It appears that American voters, in bringing the Republicans back so soon, have short memories; or maybe they were overly influenced by a biased right-wing media.

The voters forgot that the Democrats have inherited the Republicans very costly wars in Iraq, Afghanistan and covert war in Pakistan as well as a huge fiscal deficit, high unemployment, the burst of the property bubble, and a deep recession. Middle-class voters were too quick to punish the Democrats for the last presidential election campaign when their hopes were elevated by Obama, who promised too much and delivered too little. Bringing back the Republicans too soon will make America harder to govern (given the prevailing partisan politics), especially when the Republicans' main priorities are to make Barack Obama a one-term president and roll back the health care reform plan and other social and economic programs. Middle-class voters will quickly learn that the consequence of their voting will be the domination of the Republican Party by Sarah Palin and her religious-right Tea Party movement. This will mean more social division, more wars, less stability, and more political fragmentation of the fragile American political system. Worse, it will make the Republican Party less cohesive and more partisan, especially for the moderate Republicans who are now intimidated and constantly attacked from within by the vocal extreme-right groups.

This is happening when the economy in bad shape and the country in decline and in desperate need of bipartisan policies, especially in financial and economic reform. The middle class is forgetting that the Republicans' adoption of an extreme capitalism philosophy designed to make the rich richer and the poor poorer is one of the causes for the nation's declining standard of living. It will get worse as the country's huge debt is reckoned with, either through higher taxes or inflation or both. The middle class, being the easy target, will carry most of the burden in any scenario.

The Republicans' mantra of "lower taxes and smaller government" will amount to nothing or most likely will make the situation worse, especially by slashing spending when the country is stagnant and unemployment is very high. Lowering taxes, especially for the rich, will prolong the agony of the huge debt. No matter who is in office, America has to come to terms with its depressing predicament, which will continue for many years to come. US growth will continue to be weak while the household is still in deleveraging state (reducing spending, paying off debt and building up saving), housing and foreclosures are still a major problem, unemployment is very high, and the country is going through currency intervention and manipulation. America's predicament leaves no margin for error, especially if current conditions should coincide with a new oil shock or natural disaster.

For the middle class however, the impact of America's decline will be gentler under the Democrats, who are more inclined to slash military spending by ending the unnecessary wars and reducing the military budget generally, whilst the Republicans are more inclined to boost military spending by escalating the wars, especially in widening the war to include Iran; the outcome of which would likely be a major oil shock. The coming war on Iran will most likely include Syria and Lebanon. (See Chapter 5.)

The cost of America's wars is mainly paid for by the middle class and the poor. By voting the Republicans back into Congress, middle-class voters have indirectly strengthened the war-mongering extremist's political and social influence on America. Furthermore, the elections encouraged the involvement of other extreme-right Americans with the Tea Party movement, especially the likes of Glenn Beck of Fox News. The patriotic fervor created by their rhetoric and by combining evangelism with nationalism is a disaster in the making. It will result in the escalation of racial, social, and religious discrimination in addition to pushing the country further towards expansionist wars, especially the war against Arab and Islamic countries.

Beck and other extreme right-wing voices assert that aggressive Muslims are trying to impose their religious belief on non-Muslims and portray Christians and Jews as victims, which is part of a wider campaign being waged by fundamentalists who advocate the Christian domination of the world. These Christian ayatollahs are using the construction of the Islamic centre near Ground Zero as an excuse for advancing their ideas of Christian superiority and demonising Muslims.

The horror for America is the demise of its democracy, which stems from the fact that its system is becoming militarily oriented and secretive as a result of the extreme rights taking control of its institutions. In the process, an atmosphere identical to what prevailed during the Third Reich is being created, which will eventually lead to the suspension of democracy. The sitting members of the House and the Senate are not only unable to stem the tide, but many Republicans moderates are joining the chorus for fear of losing their seats. An example of toeing the Tea Party line can be seen in Senator Lindsey Graham, a key Republican on immigration reform who explicitly pledged to push for anti-immigration by amending the 14th Amendment to remove birthright citizenship, enshrined in the Constitution since 1868. He is now advocating the partial repeal of birthright citizenship and says, "If you come here illegally and you have a child, that child is automatically not a citizen."

The Tea Party movement, together with the pro-gun groups, not only want to eliminate all the moderates from the Republican Party, but they stand for war against any country that resists America's domination of the world. Furthermore, these groups, by using patriotism in their conditioning of the masses, can achieve total control of the political agenda. True American patriots, however, will eventually clash with the extremist Zionists, whose loyalty and devotion are primarily with Israel rather than with America.

It is worth noting that in response to the extremism of the Tea Party movement and its destructive politics, some moderate Americans are organising a counter-movement to bring sanity to America's political system. A good example is the October 2010 rally organised by two comedians, Jon Stewart and Stephen Colbert, under the name "The Rally to Restore Sanity." The event in Washington DC coincided with the approach of America's November 2010 mid-term elections and stood as a reply to the divisive and extremely negative and poisonous election campaign.

In conclusion, it should be said that the Tea Party movement is a combination of guns and religion; a party that wants to take America back to a by-gone era. Its slogan is "Take back America"—it does not seek to take America into the future. This is combined with much talk about "real Americans" without defining them: Are the "real" Americans the phony patriots?

Phony patriots are those who are driven by super ego and who don't hesitate about dividing society with prejudice and turning citizens against each other. How can a leader or group call themselves patriots if their behaviour results in the disunity of the nation? Phony patriots don't seem to understand that America is founded on the diversity and unity of its people from different backgrounds. Phony patriots don't seem to understand that the destruction of this foundation means the destruction of American social fabric. Phony patriots constitute the biggest threat to the country. The real patriots should expose them to weed them out before they destroy America.

The Republican Party resurgence spells a disaster for America. The work done by the Democrats in attempting to restore America's reputation and leadership role in the world following the horrible years of the Bush/Cheney administration will come to nothing. With the infestation of the Republican Party with evangelical religious-right groups, the racists, the extreme elements of Israel lobby groups, and some other rogue individuals, the party became the biggest threat to America's future. The agenda of some of these groups in the party is to push America into unnecessary wars that are costing it dearly in loss of wealth, loss of American lives, and more importantly, in creating many militant enemies around the world.

At the time of the election of George W. Bush, in my earlier book, *Thorny Opinion*, I wrote: "The election in America of the extreme right Republicans could only be achieved with the help of the Evangelical and the Israel lobby groups, as well as the right wing media and the press. The mutual benefits derived from the interdependency of religion and politics, could only be described as a backward step for America and could only lead to diminishing human rights and the devaluing of its democracy. The more entrenchment of religion in politics, the more the religious leaders are encouraged to have control and to assume the power of the state, which could lead to oppression and the desire to exterminate opponents, as was the case in the Middle Ages and in many modern dictatorships."

As it stands now, the infestation of the Republican Party with the Tea Party movement and its main driver, Sarah Palin, will give America no chance of recovery. The escalation of wars, especially the war against Islam will become much clearer and the reaction to it will threaten the world's peace.

The Administration and the Army Generals

America's unnecessary wars and the associated military surges are generally promoted for ideological and economic purposes, but unfortunately often end up in defeats. The Korean, Vietnam, Iraq, and Afghanistan wars have contributed and are currently contributing to the decline of the American Empire. This is because America doesn't understand that its military power is limited to its air superiority, with no capacity to survive a prolonged ground battles. It doesn't have the psychological capacity or the diplomatic knowledge for dealing with the conquered nations. Its generals and soldiers are trained in killing and destruction rather than in constructive human relations. The American army is called the defense force when in fact it is an attack force; its history is rich with attacking other nations rather than defending America. To save their prestige, the army generals never accept defeat; instead they plunge their country deeper and deeper into further military actions that result in more casualties and greater financial burden. The more savage the military action becomes, the more killing of innocent civilian results, and the more resentment and insurgency it provokes. Many of the killings are carried out remotely using Tomahawk missiles launched from a warship or a submarine or by drones. A drone is a pilotless plane equipped with missiles that is also launched remotely by a crew that consists of a pilot, a camera operator, and an intelligence analyst, all seated in ground-control stations on air force bases in America. Often the military announce that their drones successfully killed many suspected militants. The question which the complacent media never asks is: Since when does a civilised country kill its own suspected criminals before a trail in a court of justice, especially if these suspected criminals are often found to be innocent women and children? What happened to the Western world's conscience? Why do people accept America's lies as a triumph of the goodies over the baddies when in fact it is acting as judge, jury and executioner?

Defence analysts have long criticised drone operations because drone crews have little experience on the ground and cannot always accurately interpret raw data relayed in real time by drone cameras, but unfortunately the public reaction to the atrocities is mute.

In December 2009, for example, and as reported by Amnesty International, a US cruise missile carrying cluster bombs was used in an attack in Yemen that killed fifty-five people, including forty-nine civilians, of which twenty-three were children and seventeen women. AI released photographs showing the remains of a US-made Tomahawk missile and unexploded cluster bombs that were used in the attack on the rural community of Al-Maajala in Yemen. The indiscriminate use of cluster bombs is not only causing civilian casualties but also leaving behind unexploded bombs that threaten the lives and livelihoods of civilians for many years afterwards. Adding to that are the indiscriminate killings of women and children carried out by ground forces. This sort of aggression is typical of the way the army bombards cities and villages, which always results in huge backlash and eventual defeat of the aggressor.

No matter how much and how often the generals keep apologising for killing innocent civilians with their missiles, gunships and drones, the outcome is always the same: the rise of insurgencies, loss of life, devastation of the attacked nation, and ultimately the defeat of America.

In winning some battles, the American generals delude themselves and their country with a feeling of great achievement. With the help of their propaganda machine, they bring a temporary euphoric joy to the nation. The joy however, often turns into disappointment when the war drags on and is eventually lost, as happened in Korea, Vietnam War, and as will happen in Iraq, Afghanistan, and Pakistan. Wars appear to be forthcoming in Syria and Iran.

It is worth remembering the euphoric joy that was created by the Commander in Chief, George W. Bush, when he declared "mission accomplished" following the bombardment and the destruction of Iraq's society and its infrastructure in 2003. **Please wake up!**

Unfortunately, no politician dares to deny the generals their demand for more resources and more soldiers because no politician wants to be blamed for their defeat and because they also know that the American Empire cannot expand or survive without them. They know for a fact that a weapons-producing country cannot be pacifist. Therefore, they are guaranteed to be pampered and glorified for many years to come. Sadly, being power drunk, the generals tend to forget that a backlash against their brutality from suffering and oppressed nations is just around the corner. America's anti-democratic right-wing military-industrial complex, with its lobbying power, is behind all wars and is aided an abetted by extremist religious nationalist groups.

When the generals sense a forthcoming defeat, they turn against their masters, the civil servants in the White House, often by requesting the most unaffordable course of action in the full knowledge that their request will be turned down. This strategy usually helps them shift blame when they are not given the highest priority in funding and resource allocation. The first sign of their attempt to shift blame for their failure in Afghanistan could be felt through an article published in *Rolling Stone* magazine in June 2010. In the article were many quotes from General Stanley McChrystal's team making jokes about Vice President Joe Biden, who was seen as critical of the general's efforts to escalate the conflict in Afghanistan and who favoured a more limited counter-terrorism approach than the additional 30,000 troops requested by the general.

In the article, General McChrystal appears to belittle the vice president by responding to questions about his proposed alternative war strategy with the question: "Are you asking about Vice President Biden?" He then jokes, "Who's that?" The general is also quoted as saying he felt betrayed by the US ambassador to Afghanistan, Karl Eikenberry, for raising doubts about sending more troops to shore up an Afghan government already lacking in credibility.

In a speech in London a year earlier, the general referred to Joe Biden's alternative war proposal as likely to lead to "Chaos-istan." And he took a swipe at the president's long deliberations over the war, saying: "This effort will not remain winnable indefinitely."

Although he later apologised to the president and others for his remarks and those of his staff, he was promptly dismissed by Barack Obama and replaced with General David Petraeus.

His demise coincided with increasing frustration on the ground as the "surge" of additional troops appeared increasingly bogged down by difficulty in prosecuting the war. McChrystal's departure could be construed as an indication that he had engineered his insubordination with his civilian masters, anticipating his dismissal because of his fear of failure. He knew well that the war in Afghanistan could not be won and he did not want to take the blame; instead, now the blame will be shifted to civilian leaders. It appears that he also knew well that America cannot offer the Afghanis a better alternative to the Taliban and that losing the war will lead Afghanistan into a civil war. He knew that losing the war would engulf Pakistan and India. It appears that he also knew that losing the war in Afghanistan would reverberate throughout the Middle East, bringing Iraq back to square one and further emboldening Iran.

After all the killings and destruction in Afghanistan and Pakistan, two interesting conclusions have been arrived at, one from the CIA and the other from the British military. The CIA acknowledged there were serious problems with the prosecution of the war in Afghanistan, which was taking much longer and was much harder than anyone had anticipated and was aggravated by the serious problems with narcotics trafficking, the deadly Taliban insurgency, and the corruption of the Afghan government. The key to success or failure is whether the Afghans accept responsibility and are able to deploy an effective army and police force to maintain stability. And according to the British military, winning the war is unachievable, which is why they stated that talks with the Taliban should begin as part of the exit strategy for international forces in Afghanistan. Their reasoning is based on the history of counter-insurgency campaigns, which is that there has always been a point at which negotiation and agreement between the antagonists can be reached.

After all, General McChrystal was right; it will be a **"Chaos-istan."**

Furthermore, the Republican Party resurgence will cause the world to be a **"Chaos-world."**

Chapter 3

Israeli Cause of America's Decline

America and Israel are using money, religion, and nationalism as weapons of mass destruction

Most of the world's revolutions were led by aristocrats or intellectuals. It is inevitable that a highly equipped intellectual and influential American leader will emerge to revolutionise America's thinking. Such a leader will most likely refrain from using religious nationalism to motivate a new breed of followers. The main intention of such a leader will be to identify the causes of America's decline and its marginalisation in the world and decide on remedial actions that can put America back on track. Such a leader will most likely find that extreme Zionism is the biggest liability to America and that remedial action will necessitate the curtailing of the extremist Zionists' influence on America. (See chapter 6.)

The intention in this chapter is to highlight the peril facing the world from the use of aggression by America and Israel in their approach to international relations. Economic expansion, territorial expansion, and religious nationalism have swayed America and Israel away from a belief in justice and toward extreme brutality against their enemies and anything or anybody standing in their way. Their brutality is creating resentment and revolt around the world, especially in the Islamic world. It is a classical case of action creating an equal reaction.

America's religious nationalism is based on its belief that it is an indispensable nation, expressed in the sentiment "American Exceptionalism," whilst Israel religious nationalism is based on the fiction of the Israelis being the "Chosen People" and Israel their "Promised Land." Putting these beliefs into practice is the cause of the current conflict in the world. America wants economic expansion and control of world's natural resources, whilst Israel wants territorial expansion by grabbing Palestinian lands. Resistance by the Palestinians, who are subjected to Israel's state terrorism, seeks a legitimate base for their cause and their desire for a state. Their resistance is natural despite its being often tagged by American and Israeli propaganda as insurgency, militancy, or even terrorism. It is a typical case of violence breeding violence.

The Power of Israel in America

In his book *The Power of Israel in the United States*, the political scientist James Petras describes with well documented analysis the power and influence of Israel through its Zionist and pro-Jewish lobby on America's foreign policy, especially its Middle East policy. The book raises serious questions about the policy's benefit to America. Petras details the destructive Zionists' lobbying power to ensure America's unconditional backing of Israeli illegal colonisation of Palestine, which is causing massive injustice in the uprooting of Palestinians and the confiscation of their land. By its unconditional backing of Israel, America is pushed by the Jewish lobby into the costly invasion of Iraq and the threat to invade Syria and Iran, which is fermenting massive hostility against it in the Islamic world. Petras calls for America to review its Middle East policy to reclaim its independence of action based on its national interest. Its current Middle East policy, which has resulted in an invasion of a sovereign Arab state on false pretences, has also allowed Israel to invade Lebanon, Gaza, and the West Bank with total disregard to America's strategic interests. Many enlightened and credible Americans are now seeing that America's foreign policy has been hijacked by a well organised political lobby of Zionists and Christian Zionists. The mission of these lobbies is to advance the strategic, political, and military interests of Israel. Petras also highlights the indisputable point that most of the anti-Muslim materials being printed in America are written by individuals with close connections to Israel and are mostly Jewish.

Additionally, in 2004, Petras took note of the large number of committed Jewish nationalists working in the

Pentagon under Paul Wolfowitz and elsewhere within the Bush administration and found that they were the driving force behind the Iraq war. Paul Wolfowitz, Douglas Feith, Elliot Abrams, Richard Perle and Barry Rubin were the major promoters of the war against Iraq. They worked closely with other Zionist ideologues like Bush speechwriter David Frum to promote the "Axis of Evil" declaration to facilitate wars against other regimes hostile to Israel and America. Wolfowitz and Feith set up the Office of Special Planning, run by fellow Zionist Abram Shulsky, who used the Iraqi politician Ahmed Chalabi to provide phony intelligence on Iraq to justify that war and a regional war aimed at destroying any regime that is critical of Israeli expansionism.

In fact, the Middle East policy these Zionists formulated has resulted in America's decline. The huge American political, economic, military, and diplomatic support for Israel is encouraging the Jewish state's aggression against the Palestinians and its Arab neighbours, which is the cause of the backlash from the Islamic world. The deep-seated resentment will eventually prove to be detrimental to both Israel and America. Zionists' power in America is ensuring America's unconditional backing for Israel and the destruction of the Palestinian nation. The antipathy between Muslims and the West is the result of America's inability to sustain or even formulate a discourse related to the subject of Israeli influence on the United States. The corruption of American Middle East policy by Israel is preventing America from reclaiming independence of action based upon enlightened self-interest and progressive principles.

The question should be asked: Are the Jews acting in their own interest by pushing America into a war of attrition against Islamic countries—a savage and protracted war that nobody can win?

The resentment in the Middle East started with the creation of Israel in 1948. The creation of Israel as a nation-state, was not only detrimental to the Middle East where two-thirds of the world's oil reserve exists, but to world peace. It combined religion and nationalism, which became a major source for conflict with the opposing Arab religious nationalism. Worse still, the Jews' justification of their attitude towards the Palestinians is based on the biblical assumption of their being the chosen people, which embodies discrimination and religious extremism. Citing biblical and historical links, for example, Israel sees all of Jerusalem as its capital, a claim not recognised internationally. The Palestinians want East Jerusalem to be the capital of a future state in the West Bank and Gaza Strip.

In his book *Israel No Longer Chosen,* minister and author Saul P. Cortez provides compelling biblical evidence that refutes the long-held supposition that Israel is preferred by God over New Covenant believers in Christ. His thesis provides a proof of the horrible interpretation of the scripture by some Jewish fanatics that God has chosen people by ethnicity—which makes God a respecter of persons, which contradicts the Christian interpretation of the Bible. This can be seen in John 2:6 which states: *"We are called to be Christ like, not merely act Christ like."* It is your identity not found in what you do, but found in who God say you are. *"You are a human being, not a human doing."* And in James 2:9, which states: *"But if you show partiality, you are committing a sin and are convicted by the law as transgressor."* It is further confirmed in Galatians 3:28, which states: *"There is neither Jew nor Greek, there is neither slave, nor free, there is no male, nor female; for you are all one in Christ Jesus."*

The corrupt interpretation of the Bible by political religious nationalists for the purpose of destroying a nation and occupying their land is the ultimate betrayal of decency and justice. Certainly, the Palestinians deserve a better outcome than what they are getting, while the conscience of Western civilisation is in a deep coma.

A chosen-people doctrine believed by some extremist Jews to be of divine origin is no longer accepted on the basis of human experience, logic, and ethics. It confers to the Jews a power based on beliefs of supernatural origin and the impossible interpretation of fairy tales written over 3,000 years ago, which contradicts the modern science and ideology expressed by "We are all born equal."

What is wrong with adopting the Indian wisdom of "God comes in a form of a child," which means any child?

AIPAC (American Israel Political Affairs Committee)

For more than half a century, the American Israel Public Affairs Committee has worked to help make Israel more secure by ensuring that American support remains strong.

From a small pro-Israel public affairs boutique in the 1950s, AIPAC has grown into the most influential lobby group in America affecting America's relationship with Israel. Its objective is to ensure the continuity of America's unconditional embrace of Israel. This relationship is having a devastating effect on America's relations with the Arab and the Islamic world because it embodies the Israeli agenda of displacement of the Palestinians and theft of their land.

As America's leading pro-Israel lobby, AIPAC works with both Democratic and Republican political leaders to enact public policy that strengthens America's link to Israel. With the support of its members nationwide, AIPAC has worked with Congress and the White House on many issues to secure foreign aid for Israel, the war in Iraq, and the current targeting of Iran for its nuclear program. The influence of AIPAC on America's political life is beyond imagining, considering the fact that it represents only the extremist elements of the total Jewish population, which is only 3 percent of the total American population.

Where in the world one can find 3 percent of a population having 30 percent representation in America's so-called democratic institutions, with the ability, on short notice, to mobilise 70 percent of Congress to vote on issues that are favourable to Israel? Where in the world can one find such a small minority at the centre of America's social, economic and political stage and in key positions in the administration and in various institutions, where they can influence economic and foreign policies? Where does it leave American democracy when such a small minority, with the power of its money and subjective ideology, can determine the outcome of congressional elections? This is in addition to:

- Imposing tough sanctions on Iran
- Securing critical financial and military security to Israel each year to ensure the continuity of its capability
- Passing legislation to limit America's military sales to Arab states to maintain Israel's military edge over its neighbours
- Passing many congressional resolutions affirming support for Israel's right to self-defence, despite the fact that, in general, Israel is the provocateur and the aggressor
- Passing legislation creating an office within the Department of Homeland Security for joint research and development projects between the US and Israel
- AIPAC often supports the policies of the Israeli government with disregard to America's national interests
- AIPAC often accuses anyone or any country with anti-Semitism that dares to criticise Israel. It uses the Holocaust and crocodile tears to promote the Jewish cause and the suppression of objectivity.

Why does such an intelligent and highly educated minority tolerate its extremist leaders, who devote their energy to a destructive religious nationalism instead of constructively serving humanity? Why do

these intelligent people allow their extremist leaders to gamble with their future?

Maybe the Americans will one day wake up to discover that this small minority is operating as a cartel, helping one another gain power and influence. And maybe this small minority is hijacking America by using the power of propaganda, and using their wealth and influence to fulfil their religious nationalistic objectives. Disregarding America's national interests can have unforseen consequences, especially when the clash of interests becomes clearer to all Americans. Eventually, money, nationalism, and religion will be at centre stage of a conflict between Christian America and the Jewish state.

The recent Israeli diplomatic insult of the American vice president, Joe Biden, during his visit in March 2010, to Israel to kick-start the negotiation for a Palestinian two-state solution, was a good example of the provocation of American nationalism. Israel's announcement that it would build 1,600 new homes in East Jerusalem was a slap in the face to America, which wanted a freeze on building as a prerequisite for the commencement of negotiations.

It was taken as an insult to America, especially when Mr. Biden came to Israel largely to assure it of America's commitment to its security. He began the day on a note of support, asserting the Obama administration's "absolute, total, unvarnished commitment to Israel's security". He also said, "It's great to be home". By the end of the day however, his tone was very different. He condemned the substance and timing of the announcement of the housing plans.

"This is starting to get dangerous for us," he reportedly said to Israeli officials. "What you're doing here undermines the security of our troops who are fighting in Iraq, Afghanistan and Pakistan. That endangers us and it endangers regional peace."

A few such incidents can harm America's prestige and inflame American nationalistic fervour, which could not only harm the Israeli-American relationship but also the Jewish population in America: It could lead to new round of anti-Semitism.

The Jews, being a historically discriminated-against minority, and by virtue of their survival instinct, chose to be highly educated. They developed the capacity for achievements to become prosperous wherever they were in the world. Why would such a highly educated and talented people choose to be the cause of the next major world conflict, instead of choosing to live prosperously anywhere in the world? Fortunately and proudly, many brilliant, moderate, and non-fanatical Jews are committed to serving humanity, versus the extremist elements, who are hell-bent to bulldoze anything in the way of achieving their religious and nationalistic objectives.

The contrast between moderate and extremist Jews can be seen in the attitude of state-sponsored chief rabbi Shmuel Eliyahu, who in March 2008 called for state-sanctioned revenge against Arabs who carry out a terrorist attack in Israel by hanging their children from a tree.

The chief rabbi's extremism can also be illustrated in a ruling he issued in early 2010 and reprinted in October 2010, in which he forbade Jews from renting or selling their apartments to Palestinians. (The ruling was endorsed by more than fifty rabbis.)

Moderate secular Jews, on the other hand, were offended and horrified by the edict and likened it to Nazi Germany's anti-Semitic Nuremberg Laws of 1935. These laws and regulations were enacted by the Nazis against the Jews in similar fashion. Although the state rabbis have immunity from the law, the silence of the law enforcement agencies and the far-right government towards this sort of racism is a sign of a corrupted human spirit.

In their book *The Israel Lobby and U.S. Foreign Policy*, John J. Mearsheimer and Stephen M. Walt, political scientists at the University of Chicago and Harvard University, respectively, describe the malign influence of the pro-Israel lobby on the US government. They explore the coalition of pro-Israel groups and individuals, including American Jewish organisations and political donors, Christian fundamentalists, neo-con officials in the executive branch, and the media allies who smear critics of Israel as anti-Semites. They describe AIPAC as having an almost unchallenged hold on Congress with the power to pressure the US government into Middle East policies that are strategically and morally reprehensible and unjustifiable. It lavishes financial subsidies on Israel despite its occupation of Palestinian territories. It pressures America into confrontations with Syria and Iran. It achieved America's uncritical support of Israel's 2006 bombing of Lebanon and the war on Gaza, which violated the laws of war, including the use of cluster bombs on civilians in Lebanon and phosphor bombs on civilians in Gaza. Without AIPAC, the Iraq war would not have occurred and American support for the Israeli war against Lebanon and Gaza would've been unthinkable.

The authors have boldly gone where many other academics would fear to go. For their efforts in exposing the truth, they have been accused of anti-Semitism.

In sympathy and in total support of the two authors; former congressman Paul Findley, the author of the book *They Dare to Speak Out: People and Institutions Confront Israel's Lobby*, has stated, "I know what it is like to be targeted in this way. In the last years of my long service in Congress, I spoke out, making many of the points now presented in the Mearsheimer-Walt book. In 1980, my opponent charged me with anti-Semitism, and money poured into his campaign fund from every state in the Union. I prevailed that year but two years later lost by a narrow margin. In 1984, Senator Charles Percy, the then chairman of the Foreign Relations Committee and an occasional critic of Israel, was defeated. Leaders of the Israel lobby claimed credit for defeating both Percy and me, claims that strengthened [the] lobby's influence in the years that followed."

Findley further said, "The result is that members of Congress today loudly reward Israel as it violates international law and peace agreements, lures America into costly wars, and subjects millions of Palestinians under its rule to apartheid-like conditions because they are not Jewish. It is time to call politicians to account for their undying allegiance to a foreign state. Let the Mearsheimer-

Walt book be a clarion that bestirs the American people to political action and finally brings fundamental change to both Capitol Hill and the White House." (For more on Paul Findley, see Chapter 5.)

Reading Mearsheimer's and Walt's conclusions about Israel's influence on American foreign policy can only evoke the resentment of moderate Americans who care about the future of their country. Their basic argument against the high degree of economic, military, and diplomatic support given to Israel by America is impossible to refute. The financial cost alone to the American taxpayer is in excess of four *billion* dollars a year. This is excluding the cost of the war in Iraq, which exceeded a trillion dollars and cost thousands of American soldiers their lives. (For more on the war in Iraq, see Chapter 5.)

The Israel lobby groups have brought about a situation where it became impossible for elected officials to question support for Israel, much less redirect foreign policy in any way contrary to the perceived self-interest of Israel, including their tricking of America into invading Iraq.

The question of their power in America could be demonstrated by the abrupt retirement in June 2010 of the most respected veteran journalist Helen Thomas, whose beat included the White House, following her criticism of Israel's behaviour in Palestine. All that she said was, "Israel should get the hell out of Palestine," and suggested that the Israelis go home to Germany, Poland, or the United States. Her comments drew an avalanche of condemnation from all Israel lobby groups and the White House, which prompted her to apologise and retire immediately.

Another instance that highlights their power is the brutal attack on Lebanon, which resulted in the killing of thousands of men, women, and children and the destruction of their property. This is without counting the endangering of thousands of American citizens who were in Lebanon at the time. During this shameful episode, members of Congress were praising Israel for its brutalisation of the Lebanese civilians—and now they are expressing the desire to do the same in Syria and Iran. Israel is driving America into confrontation in the Middle East to serve its short-term strategic interests, but in the long run it will not survive, because the American Empire that is embracing it will not last; or perhaps America may wake up from its nightmare in time and decide that **enough is enough.**

Sooner or later, the Americans will wake up to the fact that America's interests are in conflict with Israel's and decide to curtail the power of Israel lobby groups in America, an action that will be viewed positively throughout the world as a first step towards world peace. AIPAC and all other extreme Zionists will then learn **"never to bite the hand that feeds them."**

J Street

J Street is a Jewish organisation founded in April 2008 by Jeremy Ben-Ami, a former policy advisor in the Clinton administration, whose intention is to reflect the views of the Obama administration and the Democratic Party.

The group is supported by many prominent Jewish members and Zionists that include George Soros, the multi-billionaire, Daniel Levy, a former high-ranking Israeli official, Lincoln Chafee, a former US senator, Samuel W. Lewis, a former US ambassador to Israel, Shlomo Ben-Ami, a former Israeli foreign minister, and others. The intention of the group is to promote American leadership in solving the Arab-Israeli and Palestinian-Israeli conflicts peacefully and to counter the extreme views of the Israeli government and their unconditional supporter AIPAC.

Although J Street is proud of AIPAC's many accomplishments, it has made clear that the two groups have different priorities rather than different views. It is at least one Jewish-American organisation that is expounding a two-state solution and lobbying against the extreme right-wing Israeli government, which is hell-bent on adopting a one-state solution by displacing and oppressing the Palestinians.

J Street is the political arm of the pro-Israel, pro-peace movement that believes in a two-state solution and urges America to help create a Palestinian state. It was formed to urge "a new direction for American policy in the Middle East, which is diplomatic solutions over military ones, multilateral over unilateral approaches to conflict resolution, and dialogue over confrontation." It believes the best way to secure Israel's future is through negotiations and peace, whilst AIPAC believes in maintaining the status quo, which is a one-state solution and the total Jewish colonisation of Palestine.

J Street's intention was recently demonstrated by its critical remarks about Israel's behaviour towards Joe

Biden and the support it gave to Secretary of State Hillary Clinton's public dressing-down of Israel and her suggestion of the possible imperilment of the US-Israeli alliance.

J Street stated that it will continue its campaign to back the Obama administration's stance on Arab-Israeli peace talks. This is in contrast with AIPAC and the Anti-Defamation League (ADL), who have unreservedly backed Israeli arrogance and who asked the White House to defuse the battle with the Israeli government and to stop demanding a unilateral deadline directed at Israel. It is obvious that AIPAC and the ADL are imposing their extreme Zionist ideology of religious nationalism on America to achieve unconditional support for Israel. It is also obvious that extremist policies will work against Israel's long-term interests. The unconditional support of these powerful lobby groups, which control American foreign policy, encourages Israel to be an arrogant state and underlines its aim to destroy the Palestinians' dream of an independent state.

In late March and early April 2010, following the clash between America and Israel, AIPAC, in a move to exploit the conflicting views within the Obama administration, has been circulating a letter calling for the end of America's public criticism of Israel and to reinforce its relationship with the Jewish state. The letter was signed by more than three-quarters of Congress. The wording is similar to an email the committee sent out during Benjamin Netanyahu's visit, describing Obama's criticisms of the Israeli government as "a matter of serious concern" and calling on Obama's administration to take immediate steps to defuse the tension with the Israelis. The committee has for years influenced America's foreign policy by targeting members of Congress. Backing down by the US administration under pressure from AIPAC has undermined the power of the president and is eroding America's credibility in the Arab and the Islamic world.

Unfortunately, because of their religious nationalism, these groups don't care about the consequences to America as their primary loyalty is with Israel. They were able to thwart the American president's effort to implement a settlement freeze in the occupied Palestinian territories, when he tried to pretend to the Arabs that he is impartial, despite the fact that he consistently pledges total commitment to Israel.

J Street, on the other hand, is offering the US administration (as a partial mediator in the conflict) more flexibility in dealing with Israeli-Palestinian problem, by favouring negotiations on the borders of a future Palestinian state, the status of Jerusalem, and refugees. J Street also favours a settlement freeze and supports anything the Israelis and the Palestinians agree upon. This belief, however, doesn't take into consideration the advantage the Israelis have as a dominant force over the Palestinians and the partial mediator (America) favouring Israel. Additionally, in December 2010 the Obama administration, to appease AIPAC, backed down and decided not to put any further pressure on Israel to freeze settlements in the occupied territories—to the delight of the settlers, who accepted this as the green light to proceed with full steam to colonise what is left of

Palestine. The settlers praised Mr. Netanyahu for rebuffing America for its pointless demand for the freeze.

This at a time when the European and the United Nations position on settlements is clear: they are illegal under international law and an obstacle to peace. What is the use of these declarations when Israel, backed by America, keeps ignoring them?

What is the use when America cannot even persuade Israel to freeze the building of settlements in the occupied territories for only 90 days as a good-will gesture to allow the peace negotiations to proceed? This was demonstrated in December 2010 when America attempted to bribe Israel with a US $3 billion security assistance package, diplomatic cover, and advanced F-35 fighter aircraft to agree to the freeze, but Israel refused. The outcome is that America's mediation effort to promote peace, its earlier promises to Arab countries, and its reputation all have disappeared. The stage is now set for the conflict to get worse. By admitting defeat in its efforts to secure an Israeli freeze on settlements, the Americans lost all credibility. America and its president appear to be weak and no match for the power of Israel. It is Israel vs. America when Israel often triumphs. **What a shame!**

J Street also unrealistically assumes that a fair and reasonable agreement can be reached between a prisoner and a prison guard. Leaving the outcome of negotiations to the oppressor and the oppressed will be fruitless without a third party's even hand between the protagonists. It will be impossible for the Palestinians, who are negotiating from a position of weakness, to achieve any long-term tangible result, whilst the Israelis are in the box seat dictating the outcome that suits the fanatical Jewish settlers. This is when any Israeli government is heavily dependant on the settlers as coalition partners.

How can fair and reasonable agreement be reached between the powerful Israel who plans far ahead and the helpless Palestinians who are busy licking their wounds? How can fair and reasonable agreement be reached when Israel is doing everything it can to frustrate the Palestinians' aspirations? This is illustrated by the passing of a bill in the Knesset that forbids any future Israeli government approving future peace agreement with the Palestinians that involve ceding parts of occupied Jerusalem without the agreement of two-third of Israel's parliament or be passed by a national referendum.

Israel is playing an arrogant game that is in conflict with international laws that leaves nothing for the Palestinians to look forward to. Israel's arrogance is destroying the Palestinians' hope and turning them into militants to fight for their dignity and survival.

Furthermore, Israel is pretending to negotiate an agreement while it continues to build new settlements on Palestinian land. The negotiated agreement revolves around the total evacuation of Jewish settlements from Palestinian territories to 1967 borders. Therefore, the only possible solution to the conflict for America to free itself from Jewish religious nationalism and act objectively by curtailing the power of the aggressor, or, alternatively, voting yes in the Security Council for an enforceable two-state solution with 1967 borders, which the international community favours.

Unfortunately, America does the opposite by using its veto power in the Security Council to prevent the Palestinians gaining any tangible results. The last veto America used was on February 19, 2011, to thwart a UN Security Council resolution aimed at condemning the Israeli settlements as "illegal" and calling for an immediate halt to all settlement building. All 14 other Security Council members voted in favour of the resolution. Mark Lyall Grant, the British ambassador to the UN, speaking on behalf of his country, France and Germany, condemned Israeli settlements in the West Bank. "They are illegal under international law," he said.

The American veto contradicts the objectives of the "Roadmap" and encourages Israel to continue settlements and escape its obligations under the peace process. Since 2000, 14 Security Council resolutions have been vetoed by one or more of the five permanent members (Britain, China, France, Russia and the US.) Of those, 10 were US vetoes, nine of them related to the Israeli-Palestinian conflict. This is when America's impartiality is the only hope for the powerless Palestinians to achieve a just outcome.

Thus, J Street's assumption that Israeli and Palestinian domestic problems are not America's problem is terribly wrong. Without a forceful lead from America, no progress towards a two-state solution will be made. J Street also doesn't take into consideration the financial and military support America gives to Israel for protecting its own strategic interests in the region, especially the control of oil supply and the maintenance of its puppet regimes' durability in the Middle East. Despite the discrepancies, J Street's stand highlights the split of opinions within the Jewish community in America.

It should be noted that J Street is another Zionist organisation supported by Jewish billionaires whose main objective is to offer maximum security for Israel, to regain the so-called "promised land," and to leave the Palestinians with a small patch of land to live on, surrounded by an apartheid-type wall. These are the same views held by Israel's right-wing Kadima Party, which was formed in November 2005 by Prime Minister Ariel Sharon following his resignation from the Likud Party. The Likud Party became a far-right party headed by Benjamin Netanyahu and is currently in alliance with the extremist and racist Israel Our Home Party (See chapter 5).

America, AIPAC, and J Street must understand that before Israel can achieve total security it is imperative that the Palestinians have a viable state, rather than endless negotiations. Fruitless negotiations were going on for more than twenty years while Israel bought time to colonise Palestine and attempted to destroy the spirit of the powerless Palestinian people.

There should be no settlement that doesn't include, first, the complete withdrawal from the occupied land in 1967, as per UN Security Council resolutions 24 and 338. Second, sovereignty over Jerusalem must be shared by the Israelis and the Palestinians, with East Jerusalem to become the capital of the Palestinian state. Third, the withdrawal from some part of Palestinian territories where Israel find it is impossible to implement, a generous compensated land should be offered as part of the negotiation, especially the linking of Gaza with the West Bank.

To ensure Israel's security, the Palestinian state can be demilitarised and supervised by an international monitoring force. The Palestinians' right of return and resettlement could be subject to negotiation and compensation.

The world should understand that radical Islamic terrorism towards the West is fueled by the failure to resolve the Israeli-Palestinian conflict. In addition, the Western world should understand that violence breeds violence, especially America's and Israeli's violence in solving conflicts. Israeli and American arrogance, coupled with their lack of wisdom and their reliance on their military might to dominate the world, is the main cause of instability in the world today.

In his book *The Arab-Israeli Conflict*, the military historian professor Ian J. Bickerton explains the root of the problem and concludes that the use of armed force has not and will not resolve the deep-seated issues that are dividing the Israelis and the Arabs.

Popular opinion, however, is that the Israeli-Arab conflict can be resolved by the West's and America's determination to achieve a two-state solution, to stop Israel colonising and annexing occupied Palestinian territories, to remove the apartheid wall, and to retreat to its pre-1967 borders. Because of the deep-seated element of religious nationalism in the conflict, medium or even long-term United Nations direct supervision will be necessary. Establishing a viable Palestinian state will culminate in all Arab countries recognising Israel and its right to exist within its own border in total security, but without the need to recognise Israel's Jewish character. Recognising Israel's Jewish character, which is what Israel is aiming for, would deny Palestinian refugees the right to return to their land. Recognising Israel as a Jewish state should not be on the agenda for settling the conflict, as its inclusion will stifle any future negotiation.

Finally, it can be concluded that the political difference between the Democratic and Republican parties is only marginal. J Street supports the Kadima Party and in turn supports the Democrats, whilst AIPAC supports the Likud Party, which in turn supports the Republicans. Both the Kadima Party and the Likud Party have similar aspirations for Israel, which is to expand and to colonise Palestine. There is, however, a difference in the degree of their extremism. Kadima is a right-wing party and the Likud is an extreme-right party, which are the mirror images of America's Democrats and Republicans, respectively. This in turn leaves no hope for the powerless Palestinians, when both the Zionist Kadima and the extreme Zionist Likud are systematically engaged in their killing, imprisonment, deportation and the destruction of their homes.

Peace Now Movement (Shalom Achshav)

Peace Now is a moderate Zionist movement of Israeli citizens who view peace, compromise, and reconciliation with the Palestinian people and the Arab states as the only guarantee for the future, security, and character of the State of Israel. The continued occupation of Palestinian territories is harming Israel economically and politically and damaging the values and fabric of its society.

The movement was established in 1978 by Israeli senior reserve army officers and combat soldiers who came to the conclusion that real security for Israel can be achieved only through peace. Since its establishment, the movement has worked tirelessly to achieve a two-state solution based on June 1967 borders. The movement is best known for its ability to organise demonstrations against the extremist Zionist leaderships and for its in-depth knowledge and comprehensive monitoring of Israeli settlements in Palestine.

It opposed Sharon's government's building of the fence (The Israeli West Bank and Gaza Strip Barriers) deep in Palestinian territory, which was aimed at the annexation of more territories and creating facts on the ground to thwart any chance of an agreement with the Palestinians, rather than what Sharon claimed, that the fence was to assure the security of Israeli citizens. The Sharon government's building of the wall was designed to imprison millions of Palestinians and destroy their livelihood, thus encouraging them to emigrate from Palestine.

The movement views the illegal outposts and the Jewish settlements as major obstacles to ending the occupation and promoting an agreement, as well as contradicting Israel's national interest. It is committed to a public campaign to evacuate the outposts and settlements while providing the settlers with adequate compensation and seeing to their resettlement elsewhere. The presence and expansion of settlements in the occupied territories and in East Jerusalem is corrupting the process of a political agreement and is a major obstacle facing the establishment of a viable Palestinian state.

The movement is not only active amongst the Israeli public, but also engaged in dialogue and joint activities with the Palestinian Peace Coalition, which is composed of political and public figures as well as grassroots activists from both the Israeli and Palestinian sides. Its mission is to ensure that both Israelis and Palestinians embrace the final solution to the conflict. Its other mission is to promote peace and democracy through education of the Israeli public and concerned citizens worldwide. In the meantime, it supports the right of Israel to exist within secure borders and for its neighbours to have the same right.

It is worth noting that the Israel Peace Now movement is supported by an equally progressive movement in America called Americans for Peace Now (APN) that was established in 1981 to mobilise support for the Israeli peace movement. It has since developed into the most prominent and moderate American Jewish Zionist organisation working to achieve a comprehensive political settlement to the Arab-Israeli conflict. It is a nonpartisan organisation with a nonpartisan mission. APN also engages in grassroots political activism and outreach to the Jewish American and Arab American communities, opinion leaders, university students, and the public at large.

Chapter 4

Economic Cause of America's Decline

Extreme Capitalism

America's extreme capitalism is diagonally opposite extreme socialism; and both are destined to collapse. Extreme capitalism is fundamentally based on the creation of economic power through political power, implemented by the middle class, to exploit the masses and other nations. It has a built-in self-destruct mechanism called *excess credit*. Excess credit extends to carry-trade, where major banks and hedge funds borrow from countries with low interest rates, like Japan, and use the money to buy high-yielding currencies, like Australia. Shifting money between countries is usually accompanied with speculations to benefit a few at the expense of many investors and the targeted countries. Other aspects of excess credit can be observed in nations and corporations borrowing well in excess of what they earn, which ultimately results in defaults. Often excess credit extends to the average citizen, with similar outcome. Excess borrowing often results in financial crisis because the survival of the capitalist system depends on spending, and when the spending stops, so does the system.

Big spending that is fuelled by financial engineering for the benefit of a few, as in the recent financial disaster, will force many countries, especially America and in Europe, to stabilise their debt. To fund their liability, they resort to printing money to revive their economies, which sets the ground for a new round of inflation and possibly hyper-inflation. Alternatively, some countries default or raise taxes to pay debt. Raising taxes leads to economic stagnation, higher unemployment, slower growth, and generally weaker economic outcomes.

In its quest for profit without taking into account human values, extreme capitalism creates many losers and resentful underclass social groups, which results in social instability and eventual revolt.

On the other hand, moderate capitalism is about the creation and fair distribution of wealth and not about lining the pockets of selected few while leaving behind the weak and the vulnerable to fend for themselves. In moderate capitalism, common sense applies. Governments retain the flexibility and the capacity to step in during economic slow-downs and periods of high unemployment to protect the country and its most vulnerable people from social upheaval.

Extreme capitalism has turned the financial markets into a gravy train for the executives and their boards of directors whilst investors and workers are relegated to the bottom of the food chain. This greed will eventually lead to the destruction of the American style of extreme capitalism. A system that is capable of producing financial institutions such as JP Morgan, Goldman Sachs, and Lehman Brothers, which indulge in rigging the markets without fear and for maximum gains for its elite managers has no chance of survival. A system grew in which large banks and corporations that expected to be bailed out by the government were encouraged to take bigger risks—which results in greater damage.

A by-product of such a system is the generated greed and the unfair distribution of wealth, which was magnified by the recession that showed the widening of the gap between the rich and the poor. It also showed America to have the greatest disparity between the rich and the poor of all industrialised nations.

The gap and its causes has been described in *Slate* magazine by the writer Timothy Noah and analysed by Professor Roderick Harrison of the Joint Center for Political and Economic Studies.

Based on census data, since 1979, incomes have been growing less and less equal between the top 20 percent of earners and the bottom 20 percent of earners. The underlying cause for the divergence was the gains in productivity that have been diverted more towards corporate earnings and profits than towards workers and employees. When the gain goes to profit and into the salaries of the top 1 percent of the population, wages and salaries of the rest of employees don't increase proportionately and workers don't get the benefit, which causes their income to stagnate. The recession has exacerbated the problem and resulted in a huge surge in the poverty rate and the destruction of middle-class income. Worse still, because of the great divergence, the stagnation of middle-class income will have a major impact on America's future growth. History shows that the destruction of the middle class in any country has always had a long-term destructive effect on its economy. All this destruction is carried out to satisfy the greed of a select few who promote extreme capitalism and sponsor extreme politicians to prevent the fair distribution of wealth. They prevent or corrupt any regulation that may interfere with their selfish endeavour.

The recently imposed regulations (watered down as a compromise to satisfy the Republicans) that are designed to curb the damaging activities of the financial institutions will have only a temporary success, and only for the period during which America and the rest of the world are in recession. The regulations have stopped short of allowing regulators to break up banks in an orderly manner when they fail. Besides, what is the use of having comprehensive regulations when the regulators don't have enough resources to supervise and control outcomes? Additionally, based on past experiences, during the next round of growth and prosperity, when the memories of the global financial crisis have receded, the regulations will be ignored. Then these smart financial institutions will develop new sets of logarithms and mathematical models—which can only be understood and administered by them, rather than by the public or politicians. People usually wake up to them only after the next crash.

Furthermore, the regulators themselves usually turn into day-dreamers when everything around them is rosy or when they don't dare to interfere with economic momentum. Under extreme capitalism, this is what happened in the past and is what will happen in the future, especially for the Republicans' version that is based on the dogmatic belief of a free market that regulates itself. Unfortunately, the Republicans' belief doesn't take into consideration the reckless behaviour of the financial sector and Wall Street generally.

During prosperous times, nobody cares about mathematical models because everybody is happy making money. People and governments usually wake up when the shit hits the fan and everything turns messy. This will happen again when a new Wall Street model is invented and optimised by the likes of Goldman Sachs and JP Morgan. Additionally, judging by the maximum 10 percent success rate of the regulators in their endeavour to pin down malpractices by major companies and investment banks, the future doesn't look encouraging. Many US court cases have detailed unsavoury trading practices involving speculation and markets manipulation, especially in the commodities markets, but the courts can offer little help in the absence of regulations, especially for high-frequency algorithmic trading. (Algorithmic strategies are based on quantitative analysis used by financial institutions and hedge funds in large transactions).

Effectively, the regulator has a doubtful supervisory power to control this kind of monopolistic trading system.

The technologically charged and highly profitable world of high-frequency trading by some investment banks represents a great danger to the world's financial system and market stability generally. Shareholders lost a level playing field in the battle against ultra-fast computers that can make trading decisions in milliseconds or, some say, in nanoseconds. Additionally, investment banks engage in proprietary trading, which is when a firm trades for direct gain instead of commission dollars. Essentially, it is when the bank profit from direct trading rather than from commissions for processing trades for clients. Firms that engage in proprietary trading believe that they have a competitive advantage that enables them to earn excess returns. Their excess earning from high-frequency trading is achieved at the expense of other institutional and average investors through speculative trading. For instance, in milliseconds they can be ahead of the queue in buying and selling stocks as their ultra-fast computers predict the trading trend between sectors. It is all legal and the regulator is powerless to stop it. **It is the mad, mad West!**

The future will be less encouraging when the Republican Party returns to the White House and in total control of Congress. Despite all compromises, only three Republican senators voted with the Democrats for the Financial Regulation Bill to increase regulations on banks and financial institutions.

Therefore, it is easy to imagine the consequences of the return of a party that is driven by the Wall Street lobby, which sees legislation as burdensome. Wall Street lobby complains about regulations that are intended to close loopholes and require greater transparency and accountability for hedge funds, mortgage brokers, and payday lenders and arcane financial instruments called derivatives, such as credit default swaps, futures contracts, options, naked calls, etc. The legislation is meant to rein in risky big bank practices blamed for the 2008 global economic melt-down and to give consumers stronger protection. It is understandable why the legislation was vehemently opposed by the Wall Street lobby and the financial services industry; they merely reflect the extreme greed of the executives.

In due course these executives will use all their skills and their lobbying power to corrupt and water down the effect of any legislation that is in conflict with their interests. Furthermore, the big financial institutions operate internationally, and without fool-proof international coordination they have the capacity to corrupt the international financial system to achieve their objectives.

It is unfortunate for America to have the Republican Party, which believes that capitalism means everybody must fend for themselves, a philosophy that is based on the principle of sink or swim. Their concept of capitalism means the disadvantaged and the unemployed who are left behind have to fend for themselves without a safety net. This can be observed in the Republicans' resistance to the Democrats' health care plan designed to insure 32 million disadvantaged or poor people (out of the total 51 million uninsured). The Republicans' attitude towards the disadvantaged can also be highlighted by the fact that over 14 percent of Americans live below the poverty line, a total of 43 million people.

Extreme capitalism is based on extreme greed and moderate capitalism is based on moderate greed—a "give and take" principle. For capitalism to succeed, a moderate greed should be taught at an early age through intelligent conditioning by either suppressing the hormonal effect or accelerating the natural genetic influence on instinct, desire, urge, and motivation. It is idealistic to fight greed and to brand it as guilt, since it is part of human nature and the human survival instinct. It is natural for the human to be motivated by beauty, dignity, a desire for security, and happiness. It is also natural for the human to want more than a fair share. There should be a legitimate way, however, for wanting and possessing things and the desire for status, provided it is based on a win–win principle. This can be achieved by self-understanding and the understanding of others based on knowledge and behavioural science, and should be part of school curricula.

Extreme capitalism also means the creation of few banks and other multi-national institutions that are "too big to fail": Goldman Sachs, Bank of America, American International Group (AIG), JP Morgan, Citibank, and others. The main objective of these institutions is to make their mangers richer by all means possible without regard to the country's financial future or their own clients' success or failure. The scandalous bonuses these managers receive are mind-boggling. These were detailed in Kenneth Feinberg's report of July 2010, which detailed the eye-popping size of the bonuses received by these managers and singled out some 600 greedy executives for using dubious criteria in awarding huge sums from the taxpayer-funded bailout money.

In today's global economy, these big banks, hedge funds and other traders, especially private equity funds, are highly leveraged (in some cases, more than twenty times their equity) and they attack markets in unison by targeting the same victims or the currency of the same country. Currencies of some countries could fluctuate by 10 percent in just a few days. This increases the risk when all of them want to take profit or to limit losses simultaneously from the same targets. In the process, governments and company directors lose control of their financial systems, which often results in market collapse, especially for the use of the modern technology of super-computers that can process trades in milliseconds. The new generation of electronic exchanges are changing the face of trading worldwide with an emphasis on ultra-high-frequency trading that can process more than 30,000 manipulated trades per second, which leaves no chance for any CEO and CFO to exercise reasonable financial control of their companies. This in turn destroys the spirit of investment and will become the catalyst for the next bubble and the next global financial crisis. An example of what might happen during multiple high-frequency-trading that caused the computer "flash crash" on Wall Street in May 2010, when over one trillion US dollars wiped out of the value off US stocks in one day.

Dealing with derivatives, high-frequency trading, market manipulation, and credit default swap that allows banks and hedge funds to wager on whether a company or a country might default, is a recipe for disaster. Employing many devices for the sole purpose of avoiding and corrupting the regulatory system of America and other countries is what extreme capitalism leads to, especially when the technology used by the financial institutions is well ahead of legislation and regulatory action.

This is one of the major problems associated with extreme capitalism, not only because of the partisan approach of Republicans and Democrats, but also because the financial institutions will always be smarter than the regulator. Market manipulation will always create high financial risk and will often lead to a major economic crisis.

Before the last global financial crisis, extreme capitalism allowed the commercial banks to become investment banks, which enabled them to deal with derivatives and to trade outside the regulations by removing the bulk of their dealings outside their balance sheet and transferring the risk to the unregulated insurance sector. This in turn created the contagion in the event of insurance companies' collapse that resulted in the domino effect and the collapse of the financial system.

And as witnessed earlier, high-frequency trading measured in milliseconds can occasionally move beyond human control and has the capacity to harm investors and other countries. Any glitch can trigger a huge amount of margin calls, markets volatility, and liquidity risk.

America's Financial Institutions

The failure of the international financial institution Lehman Brothers rocked the global economy and was one of the signals that heralded the global financial crisis (GFC).

Wall Street insider Lawrence G. McDonald, in his book *A Colossal Failure of Common Sense: The Inside Story of the Collapse of Lehman Brothers*, answers some of the questions of why Lehman Brothers was allowed to fail. McDonald reveals the culture of arrogance, ambition, greed, and brilliance, typical of Wall Street that ignites prosperity as well as the occasional destruction of wealth. It was the addiction to growth and greed that resulted in the destruction of America's oldest investment bank. Its destruction in 2008 was a pivotal event that led to the GFC and served a major blow to America's extreme capitalism, which manifests itself in high leverage, extreme greed, lies, and deception. The same story lies behind the collapse of WorldCom and Enron as well as that of future collapse of Goldman Sachs, JP Morgan, and Wall Street generally.

McDonald also said that Lehman Brothers' bankruptcy was ten times the size of Enron and bigger than WorldCom, Enron, and Adelphia combined and has made the Lehman Brothers executives subject to criminal investigation.

The GFC has exposed the weakness in the American-style capitalist system, which forced many Western governments to adopt a semi-socialist system to bail out banks and large companies that are essential to their economies. This has resulted in huge demand for sovereign funds that will take years before returning to normal and before public capital is replaced by private capital.

America's sovereign debt burden is now worse than Britain's debt after World War II, when it ceased to be the British Empire. Ceaseless American borrowing will eventually results in drastic fall of the US dollar, which will sooner or later cease to be the world's default currency. This is most likely to happen sooner rather than later, especially with the growing discontent of countries investing in America, because their investments lose value when the American dollar is low and inflation edge higher. This is mainly a consequence of the Federal Reserve's quantitative easing, which manifests itself in the injection of liquidity through buying government and private-sector bonds. The recent sustained rise in the price of gold is the first sign that the market is anticipating higher inflation and lower value of the US dollar.

As former Federal Reserve Chairman Alan Greenspan recently said, "Gold is the canary in the coal mine, which means it signals problems with respect to currency markets. The big rise in the price of gold could also be read as a new bubble in the making, and the bursting of such a bubble will precipitate another global financial crisis. It is however, the next financial crisis that will be caused by the ultra-greedy capitalists who don't know the difference between the right ways to make money from the wrong ways.

This can be seen before the GFC in the way Goldman Sachs executives traded email messages saying they would make "some serious money" betting against the housing markets. Other messages released by the US Senate

Permanent Subcommittee on Investigations read, "We lost money initially; but we later recovered by making negative bets." Negative bets known as short positions, to profit as housing prices plummeted. (Short position means the sale of borrowed security, commodity or currency with the expectation that the asset will fall in value.) And another email reads, "Of course we didn't dodge the mortgage mess; we lost money, but then made more than we lost because of shorts."

The Senate subcommittee estimated that Goldman Sachs made almost US $4 billion by betting against mortgage-related securities as the housing market collapsed. Other email messages revealed at the hearing clearly indicate Goldman's awareness of what was happening. One of the messages reads, "It is no wonder that people are fearful of this and other similar financial institutions, managed by extreme Jewish capitalists are capable of causing a devastating financial crisis for their selfish gain." And another, "But a free market was never meant to be a free license to take whatever you can get, however you can get it." And another, "Some on Wall Street forgot that behind every dollar traded or leveraged, there is [a] family looking to buy a house, pay for an education, open a business, or save for retirement. What happens here has real consequences across our country."

It is worth noting that Gary Cohn, a shining star of extreme capitalism and the president of Goldman Sachs, was earlier the manager of Goldman's global commodities and security units. He was accused of playing a major role in the Greek government's attempts at concealing and deferring debt in order to meet criteria for inclusion in the Euro zone by obscuring billions in debt from the budget's supervisors in Brussels.

Greed brings with it the erosion of ethics and the corruption of human relations. Capitalism is good, if people and governments don't spend more than they have or at least adhere to an affordable borrowing. Too much borrowing, especially against inflated assets' prices, is a recipe for financial crisis. It appears that the simple historical lesson, "excessive greed is destructive" is one that human beings are incapable of learning. It is the ultra-greed that is fuelling a silent revolution as Americans continue to lose their jobs and homes and as millions of people cannot find work or become underemployed, struggling to survive at minimum-wage jobs. Goldman Sachs, which is considered the smartest, greediest, and most dangerous investment bank (together with a few other major American financial institutions) is at the head of the cartel that is causing this calamity. It is their admission of guilt that requires the pursuit of justice and should be treated as domestic and international terrorism; not with deadly guns, but with deadly money. In their pursuit of money, they have destroyed the nation's wealth and created many victims, all to line their own pockets.

Goldman Sachs settled the claim and paid the penalty imposed by the US Securities and Exchange Commission for defrauding investors and misleading them into buying toxic mortgage-related securities just before the US housing market collapse. It paid US $550 million in fines and restitution over a structured mortgage transaction that produced big gains for one client but big losses for another. This is in addition to creating and selling collateralised debt obligations linked to subprime mortgages in 2007 when they were fully aware that the US housing market was faltering, and without disclosing it to the market. This is despite the enforceable principles of securities laws, which call for full disclosure, honest treatment, and fair dealing; Goldman Sachs was selling securities linked to subprime mortgages without telling investors that the investments would fail. Worse still, according to Professor John C. Coffee of Columbia Law School, is that before the onset of the financial crisis Goldman Sachs offloaded a lot of toxic products onto their clients and generally made their profits from trading against their customers.

While the penalty struck between Goldman Sachs and the SEC marks the largest ever levied by the regulator against a bank, it represented a mere two weeks of work for Goldman Sachs and was almost half the size of analysts' expectations.

Goldman's excesses took place when the Republicans were in the White House, and despite being a believer in extreme capitalism, Senator John McCain at the Senate hearing said, "There's no doubt their behaviour was unethical and the American people will render a judgment, as well as the courts."

Goldman Sachs and other top American financial institutions have converted the financial markets into a gambling casino and created some associated toxic assets through corrupt financial practices of derivatives trading, such as credit default swaps, which brought America and the rest of the world to near economic depression. They created a financial crisis that has driven many countries to cut spending and increase taxes to pay debt, to balance budgets, to avoid banking crisis, and to avoid defaults on loans. Ultimately, the purchasing power of many nations will be drastically reduced, which in turn will limit their growth and productivity, which will reflect on world growth and trade. It will ultimately lead to a global economic stagnation and further recessions. This will be accompanied by default of some countries that carry huge debt.

On a smaller and local scale, America has produced stockbrokers who left many investors high and dry through pressure and speculative sales of worthless stocks. From compliance documents released by the regulators, it can be seen how some stockbrokers acted with total disregard to the interest of their clients. These stockbrokers profited extensively during 2007 when investors were saddled with high stock broking charges, had little guidance to make informed decisions, and in many instances were badly misinformed, which led them to lose everything. This was called a "boiler room" trade. Boiler room is American slang for a high-pressure brokerage selling worthless stock.

Budget Deficit

America is a country catastrophically in debt; its huge debt could cripple its future as a superpower. America became an empire when other countries became indebted to it and now it is the reverse—its debt to the world amounts to over $14 trillion as of January 2011. After World War II, America and the Soviet Union became the new empires as Britain and France becoming heavily indebted. Today, America is heavily indebted to many countries, especially to China and the oil-rich Arab countries. The huge debt it carries will either drive it to bankruptcy or at least reduce it to economic and social basket case. Its political and social realities contradict its financial reality; unemployment, for example, requires fiscal stimulus, whilst the budget requires fiscal restraint, but the two are irreconcilable. Governments cannot withstand the upheaval resulting from spending cuts when revenues are limited, which results in higher unemployment and a stagnated economy. Cutting spending on education and infrastructure, for example, can have long-term devastating effect on the country's future growth and sustainability.

Adding to America's woes is its huge spending on security, the financing of three wars (Iraq, Afghanistan and a covert war in Pakistan), the aging population, and the need to raise taxes either directly or indirectly, which will further slow the growth of income, slow the economy, and disrupt the investment in innovations. This compares negatively with many emerging economies that have budget surpluses, higher productivity, leaner production techniques, and a cheaper labour force, which gives them the advantage of price competitiveness.

It is worth noting that the wars in Iraq, Afghanistan and the covert war in Pakistan were initiated by the Republican

Party on borrowed money, which was one of the main causes of America's huge budget deficit. Borrowing money to fight wars causes the country to lose on three fronts: First, the loss of the country's wealth and its soldiers. Second, the reduction of future capacity for growth because education, health, and infrastructure projects lose their priority in favour of trillions of dollars spent on military operations. Third, the destruction of America's middle class because of the country's high debt, which limits its capacity to provide incentive; which is coupled with the unfavourable taxation system that penalises the middle class.

The middle class in any country contains the brain power of the nation and when the nation's brain is sedated, the whole country is sedated. The disappointment of the middle class with the Obama administration is a reflection of the country's moving towards stagnation. The middle class that was inspired by Obama's eloquent speeches before the election, with his promises to change things in a meaningful way, finished up with great disappointment and their aspiration has died away. In reality, America's spending priority is on its military operations, rather than on building up its middle class. Sadly, the majority of America's military operations are unnecessary and avoidable—which could be seen if moderation and wisdom were given a chance to work.

Evidence is accumulating that America is reaching a turning point and the global financial crisis has exposed it as country in decline. This is while some developing countries have assured futures, for example, Brazil, Russia, India, and China (known as BRIC.)

In a recent issue of *Foreign Affairs* the Harvard historian Niall Ferguson points out a common element in the collapse of past empires, especially the Roman, the British, and the Ottoman empires that came to an end partly because of their debt. Other empires that fell into the same category were imperial China, France, Austria-Hungary, and the Soviet Union.

Ferguson points out that all these empires were marked by sharp imbalances in their revenues and expenditures, as well as suffering difficulties with financing public debt. He draws a parallel from this fact to America's decline. Britain's debt after World War II was instrumental in the demise of the British Empire and the rise of the American Empire, which was the financier of the European allies. Through the Bretton Woods agreement in 1944, through its economic strength, America was able to dictate all conditions it needed to ensure it has the financial upper hand, and in the process, the US dollar became the world default currency that was backed by gold reserves when America owned 80 percent of world's gold. This is at the time when America became the most powerful nation on earth, both militarily and economically. Because the fighting didn't take place on American soil, the country built up its industrial might during the war, selling weapons and lending money to its allies while developing its own economic strength.

It is, however, the gradual decline of America as a superpower and its people's living standard because of its huge debt that will enhance the strength of the rising powers, especially China, India, Russia, and Brazil. These rising powers can become great powers if they maintain their trajectory of fast growth and a rising living standard.

The substantial increase in US debt associated with its ever-increasing spending, mainly on global military expansion, has now reached its limits. Its vast military budget has contributed to its insolvency. Its illusion of economic recovery through bailouts is causing it to increase debt and print more money, a pathway to insolvency and the reason why so many countries are currently looking for alternatives to the US dollar in anticipation of its impending devaluation and eventual collapse.

America's budget deficit of 11 percent of GDP has woken up the world in the same way Ireland, Greece, Portugal, Spain, and England have done. These countries are left with the choices of cutting spending and increasing taxes to pay out their public debt, or default. In most scenarios, the outcome will be inflation. Inflation usually results in devaluing the currency, which in turn diminishes the value of public debt. This is what prompts China and other debtor countries to re-consider where to invest, other than in America.

What happened to America was the result of turning a blind eye on its financial institutions' speculative investments, lack of risk assessment, widespread corruption, rampant credit growth, and a rapid rise (followed by a rapid decline) in property prices, which became a bubble that contributed to the GFC.

In a tough message to Wall Street financial barons, the American people, and Republicans who oppose his financial reform plan, Barack Obama said, "It is essential to avoid repeating the mistakes of the economic crisis. The US is doomed if financial reform bid fails. A free market is not a license for unfettered corporate greed."

Unfortunately, America's financial institutions are too power-corrupt and too greedy to listen to any words of wisdom. The financial industry has become an unaccountable racket; a game in which a handful of people are lavishly paid to mislead and exploit consumers and investors. Fortunately, in modern times, the world will not be paying for America's decline and the failure of its financial system, because recent recessions have demonstrated that major economies are now less dependent on its recovery. The rise in consumption as a result of higher living standards in BRIC (Brazil, Russia, India, and China) countries and in other emerging economies makes the world less dependant on America's economic strength, which essentially means that America is becoming less of a relevant economic powerhouse and that its decline may have little impact on world economic growth.

Under current projections, America's debt to GDP ratio will reach an all time high within the next fifteen years. Some economists predict that by that time, America will be broke.

According to the International Monetary Fund report of July 2010, for America to close the fiscal gap requires a permanent annual fiscal adjustment equal to about 14 per cent of its GDP. This means, from the revenue side, the doubling of personal and corporate taxes to achieve sufficient surpluses to close the gap of its long-term liabilities. According to Herb Stein, chairman of the Council of Economic Advisers under former President Richard Nixon, "Something that can't go on, will stop." Unfortunately, it will stop too late, and in a crash, because 14 per cent of GDP is an interest on the debt. If it is not paid this year, it will be added to the next year's, which will require more spending cuts and higher taxes. This leads to a vicious circle and means that the debt will continue to spiral out of control.

Additionally, America will suffer the consequences of the destruction of its middle class and the brain-drain that accompanies it. Earlier prosperity attracted many bright people to America from all over the world. Many brilliant people came to America in search of a better future in the land of opportunity when opportunity was limited in their own countries. This is when America was embracing education and offering big incentives to attract an army of brilliant brains that contributed to its growth and superiority. With its economic decline, however, these brilliant brains will gradually move to other economically rising developed and developing countries where they are in high demand and where more incentives are on offer.

The American decline has already started, not only because of federal budget problems, but also because some American states are near bankruptcy. Many of America's states have no option but to cut their spending further, which will create more unemployment but provide no immediate solution to their woes.

With interest rates near zero, the US Federal Reserve has no option for stimulating the economy but to resort to quantitative easing (printing money) and investing in long-term Treasury bonds. (Printing money is part of monetary policy aimed at preventing deflation and doesn't mean to literally print money; it is all done electronically.) Quantitative easing is a monetary policy used by central banks to increase the supply of money in an economy when the bank interest rate is near zero. Central Bankers do that by crediting their own account with money they have created out of nothing and then purchase financial assets, including government bonds, mortgage-backed securities, and corporate bonds. This practice, according to economists, could ultimately result in hyper-inflation and lead to the collapse of US dollar. Printing money is aimed at making money cheaper and may initially add to deflationary pressure, because it creates incentive for consumers and businesses to defer purchases in the expectation of prices getting lower. Persisting with lower rates and quantitative easing, however, can result in the entrenchment of deflation, which can lead to stubborn economic stagnation. It is the repeat of the Japanese experience. (The similarity with Japan is that the economic growth flatlined in spite of extremely low interest rates. The Japanese also engaged in substantial fiscal stimulus, instituted a quantitative easing/zero interest-rate policy and created bank recapitalisation plan, which is the same what America did. Despite all the measures the Japanese GDP remains below the level that prevailed at the start of the recession in 1992.)

Creating an incentive for people to spend and corporations to invest and expand can be achieved by raising inflation expectation. Corporations that are sitting on cash will think that their cash is going to be worth less in future, hence the incentive to spend on good investment projects. This could also encourage the borrowing and economic expansion. The alternative of keeping inflation near zero results in higher unemployment and further economic stagnation that could last another twenty years. Twenty years of stagnation coupled with the American dollar collapsing will see the emergence of a new superpower and the submergence of the American Empire.

The economist Marc Faber, author of *The Gloom, Boom and Doom Report,* has warned that all of this intervention by the Federal Reserve is going to create a "final crisis" that will destroy America's financial system. Actually, all the signs of a broke America are now very clear. A book by journalist Gary Rivlin entitled *Broke, USA* illustrates how disturbingly the poor and the vulnerable in America are exploited through fringe financing, predatory subprime lending, and debt collectors. Some companies' main aim is to make big profits on the backs of America's hardworking poor and financially vulnerable, which is another reason why the poor are becoming poorer—and it is legal. A by-product of extreme capitalism is that everybody is fair game and crooks and con artists like Bernie Madoff, who stole billions of dollars from his clients, are common. What is not common in extreme capitalist America is the common sense that the poorer the majority becomes, the nearer the revolution approaches. Earlier, many people in America had equity in their homes, but following the subprime crisis, they now have negative equity or affected by foreclosures as a result of a system that allows high risk taking which has now swung over into low risk. But high-risk and low-risk are cyclical, because they happen between generations. In prosperous time, the young generation, who are living in a high-risk and high debt-to-equity ratio, has no memory of the bad time, which will make the cost of next financial crisis much larger, especially if the Republican Party is in control of the White House and Congress.

It is interesting to observe that many people have already forgotten that the Republicans borrowed to the hilt to fight three wars (one of which is just to satisfy the Israel lobby groups). They have also forgotten that it was the Republicans who turned a blind eye to the excesses of Wall Street. It was on their watch that the subprime mortgage fiasco developed, leading to the collapse of Lehman Brothers and engulfing America and the rest of the world in financial crisis. It happened because the Republicans represent the special interests of Wall Street instead of Main Street. This attitude is reflected in their partisan opposition to reform legislation that is aimed at preventing future legal, economic, and ethical problems.

Oil Shocks

The oil crisis in 1973 was a result of the Arab oil embargo and the energy crisis in 1979 was the result of the Iranian Revolution. These were periods in which the Western nations, especially America, were hit with economic stagnation and a stock-market crash as a result of oil shortages and high energy costs.

Most recent world recessions have followed an oil shock and the next recession that could lead to a prolonged depression is when demand for oil outstrips supply. Even without an oil shock, because of the dwindling supply and increased demand, a further oil price rise will be unavoidable. The recent drop in oil prices was due to the impact of the global financial crisis, but the increase in demand, due to an anticipated new round of global growth, will see a cycle of higher oil prices dominating the economic scene. It should be remembered that the price of oil passing the $140 per barrel mark was one of the major contributors to the GFC.

Economic recovery, coupled with the reduction of investment in exploration for oil and research for alternative energy, could result in the price of oil doubling, thus creating a new threat to the world economy.

The rapid depletion of current oil sources, except in the politically unstable Middle East, and the absence of new major discoveries spells a potential major crisis, especially as the world has reached the peak in oil production. This is confirmed by Professor Kjell Aleklett, president of the Association for the Study of Peak Oil and Gas, in an interview in Sweden in 2008. Many countries, especially America, have commenced their preparation of contingency action plans to meet the predicted oil crunch. America, for example, has recently authorised drilling for oil along the country's coastline, despite the environmental risk. The risk is now a reality following the explosion of British Petroleum's Deepwater Horizon oil-drilling platform in the Gulf of Mexico. America's other apparent contingency plan is to invade the Middle East, where two-thirds of global oil and one-third of world gas reserves exist. It appears that this plan has already commenced with the invasion of Iraq and perhaps the preparation to invade Iran next. If so, America's action plans to meet the oil crunch seem very scary and indicate how much the world depends on oil for survival.

The Middle East will remain the world's main energy supplier for decades to come. The Arab countries hold more than half of global oil, and Islamic anti-American sentiment is growing as fast as the American anxiety to invade and control the region. Islamic countries' oil reserves mean that Muslims will continue to occupy special significance in the global oil industry and trade for the foreseeable future.

Arab countries, including Iraq, currently produce more than 29 million barrels of oil per day, more than one-third of which comes from Saudi Arabia alone. Qatar Petroleum produces 13 percent of the world's natural gas. Political instability in these countries, further aggravated by the American military presence, will be detrimental to oil supply and world economy. The spare production capacity of the Gulf states, especially Saudi Arabia and Kuwait, and the expected increase in Iraq's and Libya's output, will be sufficient to meet global demand until 2020, when it is due to hit 95 million barrels per day, provided that political stability in these countries is guaranteed.

Unfortunately, however, the strategic expansionist interests of Israel will prevent any possibility of stability in the region, especially when America's foreign policy is dictated by the Zionist movement that is driven by the extremist Jewish settlers in Palestine. In addition to the political instability in the Middle East is industrial expansion, the increase in world population, and the absence of new major oil source discoveries. This scenario will result in the price of oil increasing dramatically and causing a major world depression.

The GFC has helped to disrupt Israel's push for a war against Iran when America and the rest of the world were heading towards the deepest recession since the Depression. For the lack of military and financial resources, starting a new war against Iran besides the wars in Iraq, Afghan and the covert war in Pakistan became unthinkable. America was unable to abide by Israel and the AIPAC push for a war on Iran. Luckily the momentum for the war was lost and an oil shock that could've plunged the world into depression was averted. But the delay in the next oil shock is only temporary, as Israel is impatiently waiting for the first suitable opportunity to campaign for a major assault on Iran. The signal for the assault on Iran will start in Lebanon, where preparation for a new civil war is now underway. The new civil war in Lebanon is designed to divert Hezbollah rockets away from Israel during the attack on Iran, and direct them towards its internal enemies, the Sunnis and the right-wing Christian militias.

It is worth noting that the Shiite Hezbollah forces are equipped and financed by Iran and the Sunnis and the Christian militias are equipped and financed by Saudi Arabia, America, and Israel. It is also worth noting that

Syria, being a sponsor of Hezbollah, will also be targeted simultaneously.

Therefore, the world will witness a major oil shock even before America's financial recovery, which will cause its economy to spiral into a major crisis and plunge the rest of the world into a major recession, just to satisfy the religious nationalist Zionists and the fanatical Israeli settlers.

Even after the oil shock of 1973 and subsequent events, it appears that America hasn't learnt the lesson that Israel's national interests are in conflict with its own. Adopting a military approach in the Middle East, plus unconditional support of Israel at the expense of its Arab neighbours, was the catalyst for the backlash that resulted in the creation of the Islamic Jihad and Al-Qaeda. Shifting Israel's politics to the far right is in turn reflecting on America's adoption of a similar direction, especially since the extremist Zionists and the Israel lobby groups are in control of its Congress. Because of America's and Israel's use of their superior military and propaganda powers, they will be first to feel the pinch of their lack of wisdom.

The control of America's foreign policy by Israeli lobby groups is achieved by the financial clout of its members and the Jewish nationalists who occupy key positions in the administration and influence members of Congress. It is undeniable that the prominence of Jewish Americans in the current administration is a consequence of both education and motivation. But using their power on the basis of "win only for Israel" instead of "win for the Israelis and the Palestinians" is provoking major revolt in the Islamic world.

A "live and let live" instead of a "winner takes all" philosophy is the best solution to many conflicts in the world. This can be observed in Western Europe's shift to a moderate and even-handed approach towards the Middle East versus America's unconditional commitment to Israel. European countries could turn into foes of Israel and withdraw their support as its arrogance becoming a major liability to their national interests. America too will eventually come to the conclusion that Israel is a major liability rather than a friend. Even the British people, America's closest friends and allies, are deriding their leaders' special relationship. They feel embarrassed by their government's devotion to Washington. Close relations with America were necessary during the Cold War, when communism was the common enemy, but now the enemies are terrorism and the dirty bomb; terrorism that is fuelled by American and Israeli aggression in the Middle East. The gradual isolation of America from the rest of the world will awaken the American people to the threat that Israel and the nationalist Jewish groups are placing their country under.

An atmosphere of anti-Semitism is now developing in Europe, which will eventually spread to America, and then history will repeat itself. When Israeli extremist leaders talk about the Holocaust, they always convey the message in a military sense: that they will never allow the hand of evil to destroy a single Jewish life. They ignore the fact that they are practicing the same methods against the Palestinians and they also ignore the fact that they should not be giving the world an excuse to turn against them, especially in their manipulation of American congressional elections, and its foreign policies. They influenced America to destroy Iraq and now their focus is shifted towards Iran. The direct threat of a war against Iran and the indirect threat of knowing that Israel has the nuclear bomb are driving Iran to develop its own nuclear technology. (See Chapter 5.)

America and Israel don't seem to understand that placing any nation under threat of extinction causes it to activate its survival instinct. At this time, Iran's decision to accelerate its nuclear program is a natural reaction to the threat it is placed under. It was the stupidity of George W. Bush's "Axis of Evil" declaration that placed both Iran and North Korea in a position of announcing their willingness to fight for their survival. America has already slapped sanctions on business enterprises connected to Iran's Revolutionary Guard and all other businesses dealing with its nuclear and oil industries. Despite America having a limited success at the UN Security Council, all sanctions will have minimum impact on Iran because of its ties to Russian, Indian, and Chinese economic interests. Russia supplies Iran with nuclear technology and China depends largely on Iran for its oil supply. China is also fully aware that America's future control of Iran means the control of its energy needs and its economy by an unfriendly and aggressive state.

In the absence of multi-polar superpowers, Russia's approach to weakening America's expansionism is to encourage the resistance of as many regional powers as it can against America—one of these is Iran.

Natural and Man-made Disasters

The probability that southern California will experience earthquakes of a magnitude 7.0 or greater is about seven times each century. About half of these will be on the San Andreas Fault and half will be on other faults. The equivalent probability in the next thirty years is 85 percent. The Loma Prieta earthquake of 7.1 magnitude on the Richter scale in October 1989 was considered a bad one, but it was moderate in comparison to the 7.7 San Francisco earthquake of April 1906, which was very destructive. Future earthquakes could be more disastrous and could devastate the American economy, especially if coupled with unfavourable economic conditions and other natural disasters, or coincident with an oil shock.

In addition to natural disasters, there are the man-made disasters, such as the aforementioned oil spill in the Gulf of Mexico, which was America's largest oil spill and has resulted in its worst environmental catastrophe, even more catastrophic than the Exxon Valdez oil tanker accident in Alaska in March 1989 that produced a spill of 1.5 million barrels of oil. It also exceeded the blow-up of the Ixtoc1 offshore oil rig in the Gulf of Mexico in 1979. Based on an independent assessment by scientists from Colombia University, the Deepwater Horizon blowout produced a spill of 4.9 million barrel of oil before it was capped.

With oil becoming harder to obtain, extraction techniques are testing available technologies to the limits. Drilling at 1.5 kilometres under the sea imposes all kinds of problems for man and machinery. The risk of things going wrong will only increase as oil becomes more difficult to extract, and when things do go wrong, as in the Deepwater Horizon accident, they will be extremely difficult to fix or contain. Prevention and fail-safe mechanisms are the only answer, but these measures make the cost of oil extraction very expensive—and as was demonstrated with the BP disaster, fail-safe measures don't always work.

These oil spills not only have catastrophic environmental effects but also have a negative economic impact on fishing, shipping, tourism and recreation. The Deepwater Horizon spill has devastated marshlands vital to wildlife and fishing. The spill sickened workers and left Gulf coast residents frustrated and angry. Sealing the Deepwater Horizon well took five months, and it will take many years to clean up the mess and many decades for the environment to recover.

America's reliance on multi-national companies renders it powerless to prevent these catastrophic outcomes. It is ironic that America doesn't invest and own the technology for deep-water drilling and the technologies to deal with this sort of disaster; it owns the technology of drones and guided missiles to create disasters in other countries like Iraq, Afghanistan, and Pakistan.

Relying on companies like British Petroleum (BP is the world's third-largest oil company after ExxonMobil and Royal Dutch Shell) to deal effectively with a disaster that is caused by the company's own negligence has just compounded the disaster. BP and many other large and bureaucratic multi-national companies tend to cut corners and provide inadequate contingency plans in their drive for profits instead of protecting the environment, especially when the cost of operating an oil rig is in excess of $1.5 million a day.

Contributing to this sort of catastrophe is the rapid depletion of oil resources around the world, which is prompting America's rush for new finds and causing it to issue drilling licences in deep water (when the technology for deep-water drilling is in its infancy) without proper engineering oversight or adequate contingency plans. The disaster is aggravated by the issuance of a "categorical" environmental exemption to BP by the Interior Department and the laxity in environmental control, which stripped away safety and cost to bring the deep-water drilling to the level of "pray for the best." It is worth noting that in July 2010, Tony Hayward, the former boss of BP, admitted that the company's contingency plans to deal with one of the world's worst oil spills were inadequate. The spill in the Gulf of Mexico has prompted the US to launch criminal and civil investigations of the companies responsible, along with their managers. The Justice Department is seeking payment from BP, rig owner Transocean, and others. The *New York Times* reported that BP was aware of safety problems at the oil rig months before April 20, when it was destroyed by the explosion. The succeeding problems involved the well casing and the blowout preventer, critical pieces in the chain of events and each, in its way, critical to the overall safety of the rig.

The terrifying lack of care and responsibility by BP could be repeated around the world if drilling in deep water is allowed to continue. The irresponsible attitude of multi-national oil companies can be starkly seen in the Niger Delta, where oil spills have become a fact of life. The smell of an oil spill can be detected long before it is seen. Forests and farmlands are now covered in greasy oil. In fact, oil spilled every year from the Niger Delta network of terminals, pipes, pumping stations, and oil platforms is more than has been lost from the BP's Deepwater Horizon in the Gulf of Mexico. If the Gulf of Mexico accident had happened in Nigeria, neither the government nor the company would have paid much attention. This kind of spill happens all the time in the delta, where the environment and human life have no value. In poorer countries, the oil companies usually cover up the incidents or just ignore them, while the corrupt local lawmakers do not care. (Shell Oil Company, for example, as revealed in one of WikiLeaks documents, had inserted staff into all the main ministries of the Nigerian government, giving it access to politicians' every move in the oil-rich Niger Delta.)

A spokesman for the Stakeholder Democracy Network in Lagos, which works to empower those in communities affected by oil companies' activities, said: "The response to the spill in the United States should serve as a stiff reminder as to how far spill management in Nigeria has drifted from standards across the world." This at a time when companies such as Shell and BP continue to avoid independent monitoring, keep key data secret and rely on the corruption of local officials.

Multi-national companies operating in developing countries leave a lot more than oil spills to be desired, especially in their disregard for the welfare of people and the environment. The exploitation of poorer countries' resources and the destruction of their environment, which can be witnessed in Nigeria, the Philippines, Indonesia, Iraq, and India are good example of such abuse.

An example of their negligence is illustrated by the Union Carbide incident of December 3, 1984, in Bhopal, India. This was the factory disaster in which a deadly methyl isocyanides gas leak caused the death of thousands of people in one of the world's worst industrial catastrophe. Almost twenty-five years and thousands of deaths later, a court ruling was handed down finding eight senior managers and middle-ranking plant supervisors guilty of negligence. The judgment offered little comfort to tens of thousands of surviving family members and those who have had their lives maimed. The horror of the survivors was in the knowledge that the earlier charges of culpable homicide were reduced to negligence by the Indian government in 1996. The American company chairman at the time, Warren Anderson, was arrested after the disaster but jumped bail and fled India to avoid prosecution; he was flown by private jet to America, never to return to India. This sort of abuse can only lead to resentment and revolt.

Last but not least, the catastrophic events that are associated with climate change are now in an accelerating mode. In 2010, the devastating floods in Pakistan as a result of intense monsoon rain and the wildfires in Russia as a result of an intense heat wave are a good indication of what will follow. These and other extreme events, such as the splitting of a giant iceberg in Greenland are, according to scientists, linked and expected to occur more frequently as a result of global warming. The emission of carbon dioxide, the main contributor to global warming, is a by-product of the world's population growth, which in turn is a by-product of over-breeding. Population growth brings with it the rise of urbanisation, the excessive use of fossil fuels, land clearing for agriculture, and the use of chemicals for fertilisation are some of the causes of environmental destruction. Environmental destruction will bring with it a calamity, not only for the planet's biodiversity, but will threaten the survival of the human race. To date, politicians and religious leaders are the major stumbling block preventing carbon emission and population control. (For more details, see Chapter 5 of my earlier book *Thorny Opinion*.)

Chapter 5

Wars: The Main Cause of America's Decline

To understand the global power game, it is worth referring to the political scientist George Friedman's book, *America's Secret War: Inside the Hidden Worldwide Struggle Between the United States and Its Enemies*. Although the book seems to be sympathetic to America's military's perspective and unsympathetic to the peace movement, it does explain America's intentions in the Middle East. Friedman argues, for example, that regarding the strategic intention behind the Iraq War, American intelligence sources knew that there were no weapons of mass destruction in Iraq, but didn't tell the public, instead manufacturing false intelligence. Another point Friedman raises is how America places emphasis on strategic outcomes rather than principles, whilst ignoring the public anti-war sentiment.

The invasion of Iraq was a strategic move aimed at manipulating Saudi Arabia, which was hard to explain to the Americans, so instead the Bush Administration had to lie by inventing the story about WMD and Saddam Hussein's involvement in September 11 attack. (For more detail see sub-heading: War in Iraq)

Friedman concludes that invading Iraq and Afghanistan was a complex thing, but most importantly it was about getting the Saudis and other Arab oil-producing countries to fear and respect America.

This is despite the fact that the Saudis are America's puppets and don't need to fear America or Israel. To prove their usefulness, in 2002, they offered a reasonable peace plan for solving the Israeli-Palestinian conflict, which could have benefited both Israel and America and could have avoided the unnecessary and costly wars. Israel at that time was agitating for the invasion of Iraq through the extremist hawks within the American Jewish lobby groups, the Bush administration, and the Congress. The Saudi peace plan had the backing of every member of the Arab League and had the potential to become the basis for an Israeli-Palestinian peace settlement if Israel and America had responded favourably. Both however, simply ignored it. The Bush administration did nothing to solve the conflict because Ariel Sharon opposed a peace settlement and opted instead to continue with the Zionist's expansionist policy of grabbing Palestinian land and destroying the Palestinians' dream of having their own state.

In the process of colonising Palestine, the Israelis are using brutal methods against the Palestinian population, which is awakening the conscience of all fair-minded people around the world and provoking resentment in the Islamic countries that is breeding terrorism, which is making America the prime target of terrorism for its unconditional backing of Israel.

America has a choice: to continue with its costly wars and self-destructive policies or to create a peaceful world that is built on a "win-win" principle. The starting point is to develop exit strategies for the wars, to remove most of its huge number of military bases from around the world. And to act decisively in curtailing the power of the Israel lobby groups in America, to enable the establishment of a viable Palestinian state. And to focus on developing alternative energy sources instead of relying on fossil fuel, the bulk of which imported from Islamic countries. Furthermore, America needs to clean up the CIA, which is acting inhumanely, out of control, and as a government within a government.

Above all, America and Israel must understand that spreading fear through their military power can have two consequences: First, fear that can destroy people. Second, fear that can drive people, by triggering their survival response mechanism to fight.

The CIA—A Government within a Government

The CIA is not only corrupting the democracies of other countries, but the American democracy as well. It spies on American citizens and politicians, as was disclosed from communication intercept scandal. Although the CIA is largely barred from spying on Americans, after 9/11 however, as reported in New York Times on December 15,

2005, President George W. Bush signed a presidential order in 2002 which secretly authorised the CIA to eavesdrop on Americans and others inside the United States. The order allows the CIA to search for evidence of terrorist activity without the court-approved warrants ordinarily required for domestic spying.

CIA is involved in intervention around the world in covert operations, para-military adventures, the torture of prisoners, and "dirty tricks." Its agents are involved in international trafficking of addictive drugs like heroin and cocaine, from which some of the profit goes to finance their covert operations (see below). Unfortunately, the majority of US media have always worked to protect the Agency and to keep the American public in the dark about the nature of its activities.

Intervention around the world: In his article in the June 1999 issue of *Z magazine*, the historian William Blum lists a brief history of US intervention around the world, showing that American foreign policy has been fuelled not by a devotion to any kind of morality, but rather by the necessity to serve other imperatives, which can be summarised as:

- Making the world safe for American corporations
- Enhancing the financial statements of defence contractors at home who have contributed generously to members of Congress
- Preventing the rise of any society that might serve as a successful example of an alternative to the capitalist model

- Extending political and economic hegemony over as wide an area as possible, as befits a "great power."

He details America's many extremely serious interventions into many countries, some of which are listed here:

Vietnam, 1950-1973:
After twenty-three years and two million civilians dead, the United States withdrew its military forces from Vietnam. Most people say that the US lost the war. Destroying Vietnam and poisoning the earth and the gene pool for generations to prevent communism from spreading in Asia, instead achieved the prevention of development in Asia.

Middle East, 1956-1958:
America's doctrine is preparedness to use armed forces to assist any Middle East country requesting assistance against armed aggression from any country controlled by international communism. This meant that no power would be allowed to dominate, or have excessive influence over the Middle East and its oil fields except the United States, and that anyone who tried would be deemed "communist." In keeping with this policy, the United States twice attempted to overthrow the Syrian government and staged several shows of force in the Mediterranean to intimidate movements opposed to the US. It supported governments in Jordan and Lebanon, landed 14,000 troops in Lebanon, and conspired to overthrow or assassinate Qasim of Iraq and Nasser of Egypt for their troublesome

Arabic nationalism and their dealings with the Soviet Union.

Cuba, 1959 to present:
Fidel Castro came to power at the beginning of 1959. This was followed by forty years of American terrorist attacks, bombings, a full-scale military invasion, sanctions, embargoes, isolation, and assassinations because Cuba had carried out an unforgivable revolution that posed a very serious threat: setting a bad example for the rest of Latin America. The saddest part of this is that the world will never know what kind of society Cuba could have produced if left alone, if not constantly under the gun and the threat of invasion, and if allowed to control its own destiny. America's policy towards Cuba lacks the wisdom that is causing the diminishment of America's influence in Latin America.

Chile, 1964-1973:
America could not tolerate a democratically elected Marxist in power. In 1970, despite the best efforts of the CIA and the rest of the American foreign policy machine, Salvador Allende became the elected president of Chile, honoured the Chilean constitution, and was very popular. After sabotaging Allende's electoral endeavour in 1964, and failing to do so in 1970, American agents began to destabilise his government over the next three years, paying particular attention to build-up of military hostility. Finally, in September 1973, the Chilean army overthrew the government and killed Allende in the process. More

than 3,000 of his supporters were executed and thousands more were tortured or disappeared.

Iraq, 1990-1991, the Desert Holocaust:
Iraq was the strongest military power among the Arab states. This may have been their crime. Noam Chomsky wrote: "It's been a leading, driving doctrine of US foreign policy since the 1940s that the vast and unparalleled energy resources of the Gulf region will be effectively dominated by the United States and its clients, and, crucially, that no independent, indigenous force will be permitted to have a substantial influence on the administration of oil production and price."

Afghanistan, 1979-1992:
Everyone knows about the terrible repression of women in Afghanistan, ordered and carried out by Islamic fundamentalists even before the Taliban. But how many people know that during the late 1970s and most of the 1980s, Afghanistan had a progressive government committed to bringing the backward nation into the 20th century, including giving women equal rights? Unfortunately, America poured billions of dollars into waging a terrible war against this government, simply because it was supported by the Soviet Union. Prior to this, CIA operations had knowingly increased the probability of a Soviet intervention, which is what occurred. In the end, America won, and Afghani women, and the rest of Afghanistan, lost. More than a million dead, three million disabled, five million refugees, in total about half the population.

The CIA and drug dealing: In his book *The Underground Empire: Where Crime and Governments Embrace*, the investigative reporter and author James Mills describes the CIA as drug dealers. Mills documents how government agencies like the CIA, charged with protecting the taxpayer from drugs or crime or terrorists or other threats, themselves become allies with criminals and seek to profit from crime while permitting field officers to go bad, steal money, and become nothing more than officially sanctioned criminals. The book goes a long way towards informing the unaware of the danger in trusting politicians and ignoring the fact that the real world of politics is full of corruption. Mills exposes the government's involvement in illegal drug dealings to fund covert operations and provides the reader with substantial evidence to prove the existence of a shadow government that is prepared to deal with drug traffickers to meet some political objectives in the name of the national interests.

The CIA method of financing a war was learned from the Vietnam War, when heroin trafficking was the norm, and such was also applied during the war against Nicaragua. This is when a huge quantity of cocaine was smuggled from Latin America, sold to the Mafia, and the profit used to finance their covert activities.

As an example, the author Christopher Robbins, in his book *Air America* details the CIA operations in the early 1950s, when America was waging war against Communist China. The CIA and the nationalist Chinese army organised the opium and heroin trade with the Golden Triangle (parts of Burma, Thailand, and Laos) drug lords. The CIA flew the drugs all over Southeast Asia on Air America. The book was released in 1979 and was one of the first to examine the CIA's secret war in Southeast Asia and their trafficking of opium.

During the US military involvement in other parts of Indochina, many American soldiers became addicts. A laboratory built at CIA headquarters in northern Laos was used to refine heroin. After decades of American military intervention, including the Afghan war, Southeast Asia had become the source of 70 percent of the world's illicit drug supply.

Alfred W. McCoy, professor of history at the University of Wisconsin, in his book *The Politics of Heroin in Southeast Asia: CIA Complicity in the Global Drug Trade,* has documented the interactions between the CIA and drug cartels in Southeast Asia and Europe. In Europe, the CIA enabled the Corsican criminal syndicates in Marseille to wrestle control of labour unions from the Communist Party. The Corsicans gained political influence and control over the ports, which helped them establish a long-term partnership with the mafia's drug distribution system, and turned Marseille into the postwar heroin capital of the Western world. Marseille's first heroin laboratories were opened in 1951, only months after the Corsicans took over the waterfront.

In the seventies and eighties, according to former foreign correspondent John Dinges in his book, *Our Man in Panama,* for more than a decade Panamanian strongman General Manuel Noriega was a highly paid CIA asset and collaborator, despite knowledge by US drug authorities as early as 1971 that the general was heavily involved in drug trafficking and money laundering. Noriega facilitated "guns-for-drugs" flights for the contras, provided protection and pilots, as well as safe havens for drug cartel officials, and discreet banking facilities. US officials, including then CIA Director William Webster sent Noriega letters of praise for efforts to thwart drug trafficking (albeit only against competitors).

The US government only turned against Noriega and invaded Panama in December 1989 and kidnapped him once they discovered he was providing intelligence and services to the Cubans and Sandinistas. Ironically, drug trafficking through Panama increased after the US invasion.

To launder money, the CIA established banks, one of which was the Nugan Hand Bank of Sydney, Australia. According to investigative journalist Jonathan Kwitny in his book *The Crime of Patriots: A True Tale of Dope, Dirty Money and the CIA*, among its managers were a network of American generals, admirals, and CIA agents, including former CIA director William Colby. The bank had branches in Saudi Arabia, Europe, Southeast Asia, South America, and the US. Nugan Hand Bank financed drug trafficking, money laundering, and international arms dealing. In 1980, amidst several mysterious deaths, the bank collapsed with $50 million in debt.

Other secret fundraising and money laundering venues were evident during Oliver North's involvement in the Iran-Contra affair. The Iran-Contras scandal came to light in November 1986 during the Reagan administration. Ronald Reagan approved the sale of arms to Iran, which was subject to an arms embargo at that time, and used the money raised to secure the release of six American hostages held in Lebanon by Hezbollah, which was indirectly linked to Iran. The plan was for Israel to supply weapons to Iran, and Iran to pay Israel, and America to resupply Israel and receive payment. Part of the money raised was diverted to the Contras rebels in Nicaragua. The aim was for the CIA to fund Nicaraguan Contras who were fighting to topple the Sandinista socialist government. (Nicaraguan Contras were various anti-communist rebel groups, united by their opposition to the Sandinistas government. The Sandinistas were the revolutionary group that in July 1979 had overthrown the Somoza dictatorship.)

Based on US legislation, the arms sales to Iran and funding of Contra militants were illegal actions and the affair could've stayed secret had it not been reported in a Lebanese newspaper.

Other CIA dirty tricks: It is their method of assassinating individuals and the mass murder of people with drones when they always declare that they are killing militants. This is when the alarm bells should sound, because they are acting as judge, jury and executioner. Nobody knows if their declaration of killing militants is true, as it is often discovered that many innocent civilian casualties were amongst the people killed. Using drones, helicopter gun-ships, and other distant targeting of people is fraught with danger, as nobody knows if the target is the real enemy. It is often impossible to verify their claims, especially when the truth is the first casualty of war and when they are controlling the release of information.

Luckily, some information comes to light through some fearless, dedicated, and principled journalists and writers or through WikiLeaks website.

The CIA has the upper hand and has the capacity to use the lethal weapon of propaganda to corrupt people's perception and to avoid accountability. This can be illustrated in their shooting down the Baptist missionaries Jim and Veronica Bowers over the Amazon in 2001. The crash killed Veronica and her baby; this was covered up for many years.

Jim and Veronica Bowers worked as Baptist missionaries in remote jungle along the Amazon River near Iquitos, northern Peru. They were returning with their six-year-old son Cory and infant daughter Charity from a trip to Brazil in a Cessna light aircraft when the aircraft was targeted by CIA spotters.

The CIA aircraft followed the Cessna for almost two hours before opening fire. Veronica Bowers and Charity were both killed. After nine years of investigation the CIA has denied that its officers had acted inappropriately when their aircraft mistakenly shot down the Cessna. The "mistake" was part of a covert anti-drugs operation. Disciplinary action was taken against sixteen officers involved in the incident.

Relatives of the American missionary family denounced the disciplinary action against the agents involved and demanded that those responsible be sent to jail. It was clear from the evidence that they lied and covered up the information; especially the cockpit voice recorder that showed that the two CIA pilots believed the missionaries' aircraft was a drug flight but had second thoughts. By then it was too late. Mrs. Bowers and her daughter charity had already been killed by a bullet that passed though her back and lodged in the infant's skull. With the pilot wounded in both legs, the Cessna made an emergency landing in the river.

It was further revealed in testimony by John Helgerson, the CIA inspector-general that the Cessna was one of fifteen other small civilian aircraft shot down during the covert operations from 1995 to 2001. In most cases the flights were shot down without being properly identified, without being given the required warnings to land, and without being given time to respond to such warnings.

This is just another example of how the CIA operates as a government within a government. Worse, the CIA was prominent not just in drug trafficking but in helping the Mujahedeen rebels fight against the Soviet-backed government in Afghanistan. (The Mujahedeen rebels were part of the Northern Alliance, which became the government of Afghanistan after the defeat of the Soviets, and lasted until the American invasion following the September 11 attacks.) The CIA's principle Afghani agent during that period was Gulbuddin Hekmatyar, one of the leading drug lords and the founder of Hezbi Islami. (Hekmatyar was a loyal agent of Pakistan and America, but now his clan is fighting against the Americans). The Americans used him in their plan to get rid of the communists and he used the Americans in his attempt to govern Afghanistan by his Islamic party principles. Following his defeat by the Taliban militia in late 1996, he fled Kabul to the north and most of his men joined the Taliban in government. It is worth noting that the Taliban was created and funded by Pakistan and America. During the fight against the communists, the CIA supplied trucks and mules to carry arms into Afghanistan and transport opium to laboratories on the Afghanistan-Pakistan border. Most of the heroin produced was shipped to America and Europe. American officials failed to investigate the drug operations because they didn't want to offend their allies in Afghanistan and Pakistan.

Another book, *Ghost Wars: The Secret History of the CIA, Afghanistan, and Bin Laden, from the Soviet Invasion to September 10, 2001*, by journalist and president of the New America Foundation Steve Coll, gives comprehensive details of the CIA involvement in the rise and evolution of the Mujahedeen and Al-Qaeda in the years before the September 11 attacks. Coll shows how the CIA miscalculated their engagement with Afghanistan and the emerging power of the Taliban after the end of the Soviet war. He also demonstrates how Afghanistan became a deadly playing field for international politics where Soviets, Pakistani, and American agents armed and trained a succession of warring factions.

Unfortunately, training and arming of warring factions, as also happened in Iraq, is one of America's misguided methods of aiming for a positive outcome, but in the absence of appropriate resources the situation gets out of control and often the unintended opposite happens. CIA covert activities often involve the mobilisation of local military personnel and right-wing groups hired and trained to overthrow their government, so America can have a new mob that is totally dependent on it, loyal to it, and happy to serve its national interests. To achieve their objectives, the CIA employs every trick possible, including fraudulent elections, extortion, blackmail, kidnapping, torture, intimidation, and, if necessary, assassination of opposition leaders.

Israel Steals American Secrets

Under the CIA's nose, or by turning a blind eye, or by infiltration and indirect participation, Israel was and still is able to steal American military and scientific secrets. This can be seen in the ironic way that Israel became a nuclear state.

In their book *Spy Trade: How Israel's Lobby Undermine America's Economy*, the director of the Institute for Research of Middle Eastern Policy in Washington, Grant F. Smith and former CIA analyst Michael Scheuer, paint a disturbing picture of America and its Congress driven by pro-Israel lobby money, ignorance, and indifference to the interests of America. He demonstrates how AIPAC in 1984, through the Israeli Embassy, passed industrial and defence secrets, which demonstrates that the Israel lobby groups are placing Israel's interests ahead of America's. The fanatical allegiance of American extremist Zionists to Israel has constantly caused the violation of federal laws—solely to Israel's advantage rather than America's.

Smith demonstrates how lobbies like AIPAC can be dangerous, especially when they act as cartels or as a political party with enormous power but with hidden activities and loyalties to a foreign country that has conflicting interests. Israel's and AIPAC's espionage and their covert operations activities in America were well known to the government in a secret file, which was kept secret until Smith's probing into the Israel lobby covert operations, especially into diverting uranium from America to Israel's Dimona nuclear facility.

Smith also revealed that in the 1960s, the Justice Department tried to regulate the Jewish Agency and the American Zionist Council as Israeli foreign agents, but without success. In the process, the Justice Department's move unleashed election law violations and escalating intimidation of American politicians by Israel lobby groups.

Smith has devoted many years to thoroughly examining Israeli lobby groups and exposing them as foreign powers acting against American national interests, and highlighting the groups' tactics in evading justice. His sources include FBI declassified files and many specific sources.

As for Israel's nuclear capacity, it can be a bigger threat to the world's security, as was demonstrated by its attempt to sell nuclear weapons to South Africa. This can be seen from the documented revelations published in May 2010 about Israel's willingness in 1975 to sell nuclear warheads to the apartheid regime. The revelations came in a secret minute of meetings between officials from the two countries when South Africa's defence minister, P.W. Botha, asked for the warheads and Shimon Peres, then Israel's defence minister and now its president, responded by offering them "in three payload sizes" (the three sizes are believed to refer to conventional, chemical, and nuclear weapons) and also signed an agreement governing military ties between the two countries that included a clause declaring that "the very existence of this agreement [was] to remain secret."

The documents uncovered by an American academic and historian, Sasha Polakow-Suransky, in his research for his book *The Unspoken Alliance: Israel's Secret Alliance with Apartheid South Africa*, on the close relationship between the two countries, provide evidence that Israel has nuclear weapons, despite its policy of neither confirming nor denying their existence. South African documents show that the apartheid-era's military wanted the missiles as a deterrent and for potential strikes against neighbouring states. The agreement was for the supply of Jericho missiles under a project code-named "Chalet."

Mr. Botha did not go ahead with the deal, in part because of the cost. In addition, any deal would have had to have the final approval by Israel's prime minister and it is uncertain if that would have been forthcoming. It has been speculated that South Africa eventually built its own nuclear bombs, possibly with Israeli assistance. But the collaboration on military technology only grew over the following years. South Africa also provided much of the yellowcake uranium that Israel required to develop its weapons.

Despite Shimon Perez's denials of offering to sell nuclear weapons, the declassified secret South African documents prove otherwise. Polakow-Suransky said that the denials were disingenuous because the minutes of the meetings indicate that an explicit offer to supply nuclear warheads by Israel had been made and a secrecy agreement with P.W. Botha was signed. The agreement governed the broad conduct of the military relationship between the two countries, including a commitment to keep it secret.

In a book entitled *Imperial Hubris: Why the West is Losing the War on Terror*, former CIA analyst Michael Scheuer concluded that pro-Israel lobby groups are beyond dangerous, especially for encouraging US-Islamic confrontation. The explosive evidence of spying for Israel presented in these books makes the lobby groups not only dangerous, but a direct threat to America.

The long-term corrosive influence of Israeli lobby groups is well demonstrated by Paul Findley, member of Congress from 1961–1983, in his book *They Dare to Speak Out*. Findley was in a unique position to write about the pro-Israel lobby, and specifically about the American-Israel Public Affairs Committee (AIPAC) for the role it played in his own defeat in early 1980. He knows that many politicians have lost elections due to the influence of this group with its clout to defeat politicians who dare to question Israel's influence on America's foreign policy. It is obvious that AIPAC intimidates and silences any voices against Israel for its behaviour towards the Palestinians and the theft of their land. Other politicians who question Israel's spying on American institutions are sent letters and threatening phone calls, and the ones who cannot be silenced are unfairly branded anti-Semites.

The book also shows that the intimidation is not limited to politicians, but to government officials, teachers, and journalists who don't toe the Israeli line. The book highlights some disturbing accounts of Jonathan Pollard's spying and the theft of sensitive documents for Israel that endangered America's security. The most interesting part of the book is his description of the attack on the USS *Liberty*. In 1967, the technical research ship *Liberty* was attacked by Israeli planes and gunboats. It was machine-gunned, torpedoed, and napalmed by Israeli forces. Thirty-four American servicemen were killed and hundred seventy more injured. (Both the Israeli and U.S. governments conducted inquiries and issued reports that concluded the attack was a mistake due to Israeli confusion about the identity of the USS *Liberty*.

The Israeli claim of mistaken identity and the attack was an accident didn't convince many Americans. Some survivors, in addition to some U.S. diplomats and intelligence officials involved in the incident continue to dispute these official findings, saying the Israeli attack on the USS *Liberty* was not a mistake, as the ship was in international waters and flying the American flag and its identification was clearly indicated in large white letters and numerals on its hull. In statement and a signed affidavit, retired Capt. Ward Boston said President Lyndon Johnson and Secretary of Defense Robert McNamara told those heading the Navy's inquiry to "conclude that the attack was a case of mistaken identity despite overwhelming evidence to the contrary."

At the Senate Foreign Relations Committee, Senator Bourke B. Hickenlooper expressed the feeling of other senators in saying: "From what I have read I can't tolerate for one minute that this attack was an accident.")

The evidence presented by Findley in his book is overwhelming and should make every free-thinking person angry. To criticise Israeli policy is not anti-Semitism; it is merely to hold Israel accountable for its actions and its behaviour towards the Palestinians. Findley didn't deserve the insults and slurs he suffered for telling the truth. One of the truths is highlighted in his statement: **"There is an open secret in Washington. I learned it well during my 22-year tenure as a member of the US House of Representatives. All members swear to serve the interests of the United States, but there is an unwritten and overwhelming exception: The interests of one small foreign country almost always trump US interests. That nation of course is Israel."** And he further states: "On several occasions, colleagues told me privately that they admired what I was trying to do in Middle East policy reform, but they could not risk the pro-Israel protest back home by supporting my positions. The pro-Israel lobby is not one organisation orchestrating the US Middle East policy from a backroom in Washington, nor is it entirely Jewish. It consists of scores of groups, large and small that work at various levels. The largest, most professional, and most effective is the American Israel Public Affairs Committee."

American patriots, especially the redneck elements in the Tea Party, may one day come to the conclusion that their country is being hijacked by AIPAC to benefit a rogue country and decide it's time to liberate America.

The CIA is a huge bureaucracy: The CIA got worse following its enlargement after the September 11 attacks. According to a *Washington Post* report by Dana Priest and William Arkin published in July 2010, the organisation became so large and secretive that no one knows its value, how many people it employs, how many programs it runs, and how many other agencies are doing the same work. The report said there are now more than 1,200 government organisations and more than 1,900 private companies working on counter-terrorism, homeland security, and intelligence in 10,000 locations across the US. It is estimated that the CIA and its affiliates employ 854,000 agents, which includes 265,000 contractors. It produces 50,000 intelligence reports each year, a number of them so large that they are routinely ignored. The investigation revealed a secret organisation grown since September 11, one that lacks in thorough oversight and it is so unwieldy that its effectiveness is impossible to determine. A staffer on the Senate Armed Services Committee described it as "a living, breathing organism impossible to control or curtail." He further said, "How much money has been involved is just mind-boggling," and added "We've built such a vast instrument. What are you going to do with this thing? It's turned into a jobs program."

Since September 11, the US intelligence and counter-intelligence system has grown so huge that it is now beyond the control of any single official or agency. It was revealed that its budget in 2010 totaled $80 billion. It has systemic problems that prevent its branches communicating with each other. Priest and Arkin describe it: "With the quick infusion of money, military and intelligence agencies multiplied; 24 organisations were created by the end of 2001, including the Office of Homeland Security and the Foreign Terrorist Asset Tracking Task Force. In 2002, 37 more organisations were created to track weapons of mass destruction, collect threat tips and coordinate the new focus on counter-terrorism. That was followed in the next year by 36 new organisations; and 26 after that; and 31 more; and 32 more; and 20 or more each in 2007, 2008 and 2009."

It is no wonder that so many new agencies, with over 850,000 people, are unable to communicate with each other, especially with floods of information to be analysed.

Torturing Prisoners

Last but not least, the CIA's torture of prisoners or the shuffling of prisoners around the world to countries where torturing people is common was intensified following the September 11 attacks.

In his book *A Question of Torture: CIA Interrogation, from the Cold War to the War on Terror (American Empire Project)* the professor of history Alfred McCoy points out that the CIA-funded research in experimental psychology for the investigation of human ecology for mind control. The aim for the research is to identify key behavioural components integral to its emerging psychological torture technique, especially the devastating impact of sensory deprivation.

The CIA's main objective for torturing prisoners following the September 11 attacks was to find the links between Saddam Hussein and Al-Qaeda to justify America's planned invasion of Iraq.

In his article of May 24, 2009, "The Torture Memos," professor of history and philosopher Noam Chomsky details the testimony in the Senate Armed Services Committee report on Vice President Dick Cheney's and Defense Secretary Donald Rumsfeld's desperation to find these links, irrelevant "facts" that were later concocted as justification for the invasion. In his testimony, former army psychiatrist Major Charles Burney said that a large part of the time they were focused on trying to establish a link between Al-Qaeda and Iraq. The more frustrating it became to try to establish such links, the more pressure was applied with measures that might produce more immediate results; that is, torture.

The McClatchy press, (the second largest American newspaper company) reported that a former senior intelligence official familiar with the interrogation issue added that the Bush administration applied relentless pressure on interrogators to use harsh methods on detainees, in part to find evidence of cooperation between Al-Qaeda and Saddam Hussein's regime. There was constant pressure on the intelligence agencies and the interrogators to do whatever it took to get that information out of the detainees, especially the few high-value ones; and when people kept coming up empty, they were told to push harder.

According to Alfred McCoy, victims worldwide have also endured the CIA's tortures, which were highlighted by their methods in the Abu Ghraib prison following the invasion of Iraq.

This is what happens in a country that led the world to believe it was the symbol of democracy and the champion of human rights, when this is what they do and not what they pretend to stand for. It should be understood however, that this is not a reflection of the American people, because the Americans are themselves victims of misinformation and propaganda perpetrated by vested interests, right-wing media, and manipulative extremist leaders.

The Obama administration banned all forms of torture, which is a step in the right direction. This will not, however, prevent the CIA from shuffling victims to foreign countries that are governed by American puppet regimes, where torture of prisoners is a common practice. The Obama administration did not shut down the practice of torture when it could by banning the CIA from sending prisoners to these countries and by making a stand against any country that is in conflict with human rights principles. If there is no puppet regime willing to carry out all America's dirty work, the CIA will create one through a military coup to install a military dictator or through a common method of manufactured democracy or a democracy imposed under the power of the gun.

It is worth noting that following a US federal court ruling, former prisoners of the CIA cannot sue over their torture in overseas prisons because such a lawsuit might expose secret government information. The court ruling exposes the American justice system for its bias against human rights and in favour of perceived national security issues, which gives a license to the CIA to continue violating human rights. The American Civil Liberties Union (ACLU) filed a case in 2007 on behalf of five former prisoners who said they were kidnapped, transported to foreign countries, and tortured in the custody of foreign governments or the CIA. The lawsuit was against a Boeing subsidiary, Jeppesen Dataplan, for allegedly flying terrorism suspects to secret CIA sites in foreign countries (a practice known as rendition) for interrogation. The court ruling is another nail in the coffin of America's reputation as a champion of human rights.

America's reputation is now at its lowest ebb following the release of WikiLeaks documents in October 2010. The 400,000 field reports published by the whistle-blowing website show evidence that US soldiers handed over Iraqi detainees to the notorious torture squad; the Iraqi Wolf Brigade. The Wolf Brigade is famous for subjecting prisoners to pain and agony in the process of interrogation. Within the leaked archive is a batch of secret field reports from the town of Samarra, northwest of Baghdad. They corroborate previous allegations that the US military turned over many prisoners to the Wolf Brigade, the 2nd battalion of the interior ministry's special commandos, who were beating prisoners, torturing them with electric drills, and sometimes executing suspects. In Samarra, the series of log entries in 2004 and 2005 describe repeated raids by US infantry, who then handed their captives over to the Wolf Brigade for further questioning.

The leaked documents detail the brutality, torture, beatings, and sexual abuse of Iraqi Sunnis by the Iran-supported Shiite security forces, while American troops, who played an important role in making this violence happen, often looked on. Not only do the leaked documents show that American soldiers have killed large numbers of civilians, it is also clear that they did nothing to stop the Iraqi security forces from torturing and murdering prisoners. To throw sand in the eyes of the world, the only excuse the Americans can offer is that Iraq is a sovereign state. The question to be asked is: How can a country under military occupation run by the American invader be a sovereign state?

It is worth noting that the 1949 Geneva Conventions prohibit any physical or moral coercion, in particular any coercion used to obtain information.

In an article titled: "The Shaming of America," Robert Fisk, in his newspaper, *The Independent,* wrote, "The Pentagon's anger over the WikiLeaks documents was not because their secrecy had been breached, but because they'd been caught out telling lies." He delivered a searing description after the WikiLeaks revelations that expose in detail the brutality of the war in Iraq and the disgraceful deceit of the Americans. In support of WikiLeaks documents, Fisk said, "American witnesses to torture, they didn't do anything that the Iraqis-security authorities were torturing Iraqis, that American air strikes were killing many civilians. We knew about this, but it was always denied by the Americans. I was doing stories years ago about Iraqis torturing Iraqis and the stories were coming from American officers who were leaking them to me. But of course every time I wrote them in the paper, the Americans denied that it was true. I went to the scenes of US air strikes. They were obviously limbs, hands, arms of children, babies, women, civilians, as well sometimes as armed men, and we wrote about this. What the WikiLeaks does is it proves beyond any doubt that what we reported was correct and that what we were told by the American authorities was mendacious, it was a lie. The Americans now are saying-Shame upon WikiLeaks. It's endangering lives in Iraq—I mean, invading Iraq endangered an awful lot of lives, didn't it?"

In a comment about American hypocrisy he said, "I think there's an awful lot of hypocrisy here. The fact of the matter is that routinely when armies go abroad to other countries far away, they torture and they abuse and they turn blind eyes. Look at Korea, look at Vietnam. I could go through a whole lot more. And it will happen again. I don't think we care about the people whose lands we occupy and that is the problem."

As evidence of America's shame, Fisk mocks the military's lies about the Iraqi civilian casualties and gives a chilling description of the brutal treatment of Iraqi prisoners. He writes, "This is material that can be used by lawyers in courts. If 66,081—I loved the '81' bit—is the highest American figure available for dead civilians, then the real civilian mortality score is infinitely higher since this records only those civilians the Americans knew of. Some of them were brought to the Baghdad mortuary in my presence, and it was the senior official there who told me that the Iraqi ministry of health had banned doctors from performing any post-mortems on dead civilians brought in by American troops. Now why should that be? Because some had been tortured to death by Iraqis working for the Americans? Did this hook up with the 1,300 independent US reports of torture in Iraqi police stations?"

Unfortunately, when future documents are leaked, the world will be witnessing further corruption of the Geneva Convention and the repeat of the Iraqi experience in Afghanistan with more intensity by the heavily armed American troops. It will get worse for the civilians when America decides to invade Iran and Pakistan, because the resistance they will encounter there will be much greater.

It is ironic that America has always pretended to champion human rights and was always ready to criticise any country that violated human rights. It is now exposed as a country that has no regard for human rights. The army and CIA train their interrogators to aim at provoking humiliation, insecurity, disorientation, exhaustion, positional asphyxiation, sleep deprivation, anxiety, and fear—and strip prisoners naked before interrogation. This is a total corruption of human spirit.

Iran is a Nuclear State—Thanks to George W. Bush's "Axis of Evil" Declaration and Israel's Nuclear Weapons

On February 12, 2010, Iran's President Mahmoud Ahmadinejad used a massive pro-government rally in Tehran to boast that the Islamic republic is now a nuclear state and on the brink of having the means to produce enriched uranium. Even more ominously for the West, he also declared that Iran now has the capacity to enrich uranium to 80 percent, which is a fraction short of the weapons grade needed to build a nuclear bomb.

Iran also launched the Kavoshgar 3-Explorer rocket that carried a capsule containing live animals, which was Iran's first experiment in sending living creatures into space. America branded the launch a provocative act.

Iran's action is the result of shifting the balance of military power heavily in favour of Israel, who with the direct help of America and by stealing its secrets was able to acquire nuclear capability, which indicates that the Nuclear Non-proliferation Treaty (NPT) had failed in its mission to prevent the stockpile of weapons.

For years, Iran has been targeted by America and Israel with threats of sanctions and military attacks over its suspected push to build a nuclear bomb when Israel is the only country in the Middle East to already have nuclear bombs and is the only country other than America that is ready to use them without hesitation.

Israel is a non-signatory to the NPT and its nuclear facilities were never subject to International Atomic Energy Agency (IAEA) inspection regimes, whilst Iran is a signatory to the treaty. All Western governments acknowledge that Israel's Dimona plant in the Negev Desert is where its nuclear arsenal is located, according to the Jewish nuclear expert Avner Cohen. Israel is in all likelihood the Middle East's sole nuclear power. The latest modest estimate by US intelligence is that Israel has about 100 weapons, which it acquired by stealth, and it refuses to acknowledge their possession.

The credibility problem in this for America is tolerating Israel's nuclear capacity, while it is attempting to round up support at the United Nations for Iran to be punished for its nuclear program. The fact that Israel continues with its policy of secrecy and with maintaining a nuclear capability, in itself is not conducive to convincing Iran and other nations who are directly or indirectly threatened by Israel, not to develop their own nuclear capacity. It is their survival instinct that has being activated—and who can blame them?

Developing and spreading nuclear capacity in the Middle East will pose the biggest threat to America's national interests and is primarily a consequence of its unconditional support of Israel. It is easy to see that this support has turned Israel into a cancerous growth on America's body that will continue to grow until the ultimate demise of both. Israel with the help of AIPAC never hesitates to use America, its technology, and its people to fulfil its own agenda of the "Zionist project." For America, it is disingenuous to demand a severe round of sanctions against Iran for its nuclear program without including Israel, Pakistan, and India for similar treatment.

Although the imposed sanctions include restrictions on Iranian banks, a cargo inspection regime, and an expansion of the existing arms embargo, it doesn't include any crippling economic sanctions or oil embargo. It therefore will have little effect on the outcome. The solution lies with declaring the Middle East nuclear-free and disarming Israel of its nuclear weapons and dismantling its nuclear facilities.

No matter how much propaganda is applied, Iran's survival will depend on its production of a nuclear bomb to counter its two major adversaries, America and Israel, who are armed to the teeth with heavy conventional and nuclear weapons. This reality makes the Iranian claim that its nuclear program is for peaceful purpose unbelievable. The other reality is that both sides are driven by religious nationalism, which was and will always be one of the main causes of wars and destruction worldwide. Attempting to disarm Iran without disarming Israel will be a futile exercise because placing a nation under the threat of extinction can only awaken its survival instinct.

At the urging of Israel and the CIA, the Pentagon has developed an air strike plan against Iran called the "kinetic option." According to Michael Hayden, a retired US Air Force general and former director of CIA under President George W. Bush, the kinetic option is euphemism for air strikes against Iran. Because of sanctions have not succeeded in stopping Iran's nuclear weapons program, Hayden considers the air strike is not the worse option. The Pentagon in April 2010 said, "While a military strike against Iran was off the table for the near term, such action had not been ruled out." However, judging by the many interviews given by former British Prime Minister Tony Blair in conjunction with the release of his autobiography in September 2010, it is becoming obvious that America and

Israel are unleashing him to prepare the world opinion for a military solution as the only option to deal with nuclear Iran. Blair was the chief propagandist for the Iraq war and despite his credibility being in tatters, his skill in "BS" is in high demand again to prepare the world for a war on Iran. Blair, apparently a Christian Zionist, is the same man who shared the views of George W. Bush after 9/11 and said, "Everything changed and the world had to be remade and the Islamic world had to be remade."

The outcome of this rhetoric is provoking bigger threats of terrorism, which will get much worse if war is declared on Iran, which has the potential to unite the Sunni and the Shiite fanatics, as they will perceive it as an all-out war on Islam.

The remaking of the Islamic world that is being advocated by the Zionists and the Christian Zionists can only lead to the weakening of the moderate Muslims and the strengthening of the radicals. Worse yet, the remaking of the Islamic world through the Iraq war has strengthened Iran and weakened its moderate Arab neighbours to the detriment of the national security of the West. The threat to Israel and the national security of the West was caused by the change of the balance of power in the region. This is what Blair is using in his argument for action against Iran. Unfortunately, scaring the world about Iran—just as he did in relation to Iraq's WMD—is only propaganda because he discounts the fact that America and Israel, if they desire to use it, have the combined conventional and nuclear capability to send Iran back to the Stone Age in a few days. But the consequence of that is an unaffordable oil shock, and America and Europe are currently in deep financial trouble.

Helped by a biased media, in the same breath, Blair is promoting the idea that Iran is fomenting extremism everywhere and that Islamic extremism is causing the West's reaction and the rise in the West of Islamophobia. With this fact-twisting, he purposely ignores the facts: First, Iran itself is the target of the Sunnis' sectarian extremism. Second, it could be Israel's and the West's extremism that is causing the Islamic reaction. Israeli and American expansionism—their quest for land and resources—could be the cause of terrorism. It is most likely that their "winner takes all" approach is the cause for the Islamic revolt and "Westernophobia."

The West, in the meantime, in unleashing Tony Blair again, is sending the signal that the Israeli-Palestinian peace talks are designed to soften up the Islamic world's reaction to the forthcoming attack on Iran. It appears that the thought behind preparing the world opinion is: America and Israel are going for a military strike against Iran when the conditions are right. America currently has no money and is no position to start a new war while it is fighting on three fronts; Iraq, Afghanistan and a covert war in Pakistan.

The world, in the meantime, should be watching for Blair's rhetoric to reach fervour pitch; it will mean the attack on Syria and Iran is imminent. It is unfortunate that the stupidity of the constant threat of a military action against Iran is giving Iran the incentive to speed up its nuclear program.

Afghanistan War

The war in Afghanistan is a war nobody can win. American generals keep asking for surges and reinforcements, as they did in Korea and Vietnam, but without achieving final victory. It should be asked, then, if they can't defeat a hopeless and badly equipped Taliban with their sophisticated military technologies, who on earth can they defeat?

America is playing a double game in Afghanistan by fighting the terrorists it once supported to fight the Soviets. The Taliban (which literally means seekers of knowledge, or students) were the by-product of the Soviet invasion of Afghanistan, which started on December 25, 1979. They became refugees on the Pakistani side of the border, where relief and education were provided by religious organisations, which were in turn funded by Saudi Arabia and the CIA.

Prior to the intolerant fundamentalist Taliban, the majority of Afghanis, like the majority of Indian and Pakistani Muslims, Turks, Central Asians, and Caucasians, belonged to a more tolerant and moderate form of Islamic religion. Against this background, the Americans saw the opportunity in the intolerant Taliban to humiliate the Soviets. They enthusiastically encouraged the Islamic dimension of the Afghan religious-nationalistic war against Soviet occupation, which culminated in the rise of the Mujahedeen (Islamic warriors), who were then the darlings of the CIA.

Osama bin Laden was also an Islamic warrior, but independent of the CIA, Saudi Arabia, and Pakistan. The Soviets departed in defeat but left Afghanistan in a social mess and with nothing to unite the largely tribal country. Consequently, upon the departure of the Soviets, and once their puppet government had been defeated, Afghanistan was faced with a political vacuum. This vacuum was made worse by the fighting between the contending tribal leaders vying for exclusive control. In this environment of war, and with the support of Pakistan, the Taliban became involved, promising peace and stability. By 1996, the Taliban succeeded in establishing themselves as the rulers of most of Afghanistan. Through their harsh and very restrictive rule, they succeeded in providing peace and security to the Afghans under their control.

It is worth noting that Afghanistan, during the Taliban rule, and Saudi Arabia, represented the most fundamentalist interpretation of Sunni Islam and were both the only countries that were, religiously, so closed off from the rest of the world.

It is also worth noting that the former leader of the Soviet Union, Mikhail Gorbachev, has warned that Afghanistan risks turning into another Vietnam for the US, telling NATO that victory is impossible. Mr. Gorbachev, who pulled the Russian troops out of Afghanistan in 1989 after a ten-year war, said, "The US has no alternative but to withdraw. Victory is impossible in Afghanistan, no matter how difficult it will be." He further said, "Because of this, withdrawal would be more difficult. But what is the alternative—another Vietnam? Sending in half a million troops? That wouldn't work."

Now America wants to defeat the Taliban and establish a new democracy run by corrupt drug dealers and thieves who will be loyal agents serving Western interests. America is fooling itself and the world in its reliance on a corrupt democracy and leadership in Afghanistan that will be of no use to America or the Afghan people. It is an American fantasy that these loyal agents will be capable of holding the country together without turning it into a failed state, that is, unless America is willing to keep its troops there for many decades at an astronomical cost in money and lives. American fantasy will turn into a nightmare when it leaves Afghanistan to find that the majority of the new Afghan army, together with its NATO-supplied equipment, will be in the hands of the Mujahedeen insurgency.

The so-called democratic Afghani regime that America has manufactured is totally corrupt from the top down. This can be seen in the corrupt connection of Kabul Bank with the 2009 election of President Hamid Karzi and the corrupt bank loans to his brother, Mahmoud Karzi. Because of the Karzi family connections to the bank, the regulator did not examine the freewheeling and shoddy management of the bank. This led to property purchases in the United Arab Emirates at the height of the real estate market, and when the real estate market collapsed, the bank's investments collapsed with it. This in turn has resulted in large-scale chaos and a run of depositors on the bank, which brought it to near collapse. It is the bank that the government heavily relies on to pay the salaries of thousands of police officers and soldiers.

This endemic corruption extends to all other public and private institutions and is destroying public confidence and strengthening the insurgency. The American manufactured democracy is at the heart of the corruption, and the only incentive for public officials who risk their lives to serve America's interests is the financial rewards gained from being in power. America did the same in Iraq. They think that the only way to succeed in these countries is to buy a regime that becomes loyal to them by allowing the officials of such a regime to enrich themselves illegally and at the expense of the poor population. This is why Afghanis prefer a cleaner Taliban regime, and that is why America will never succeed, even if they install a new government, as they did in Vietnam.

A change of government appears certain because, first, the Karzi government is totally corrupt and becoming an embarrassment to America and its allies. Second, America's allies are becoming hesitant to continue with a war that is costing them too many casualties and which at best will result in a civil war and finally a failed state. Third, Hamid Karzi is openly telling the truth by criticising America in its way of fighting an insurgency that is producing nothing but civilian casualties, which is only adding to the anti-American sentiment.

Karzi is right, because since the start of the war in Afghanistan, the fighting in the villages has been ineffective, apart from causing civilian deaths. However, in the eyes of the Americans, Karzi is committing a cardinal sin in criticising the masters who installed him as a president to serve their strategic interests. Karzi should be saying what the Americans don't understand that putting an Afghan face on this war is difficult when members of the various ethnic groups that make up Afghanistan are deeply divided and the only groups that can hold the country together are the Pashtuns who were governing Afghanistan since its founding in 1747. The Pashtuns are the majority of the nation and are loyal supporters of the Taliban. Despite the propaganda, it will be impossible for the Americans to win over Afghanis hearts, first because they are considered the infidel and second, because of the collateral damage and the killing of civilians, which provokes hatred and deepens the feeling for revenge. Civilian casualties in such a war are caused by, among other things, the difficulty in distinguishing between the insurgents and the civilians, especially for the indiscriminate bombardment of targets by remote air-strikes, drones, and helicopter gunships.

Following the release of Iraq's Secret War files and the Afghan War diary by WikiLeaks, former CIA field officer in the Middle East Robert Baer, the author of books, *See No Evil, The Devil We Know: The True Story of Ground Soldier in the CIA's War on Terrorism,* and *Blow the House Down: A Novel* wrote, "The release of the secret reports has uncovered major flaws in the US military campaign, including that the information being used to justify deadly raids is fragmented and largely coming from secondary sources." He further wrote, "Much of the information appears to be from intelligence peddlers who are looking for a reward for passing on gossip and there is nothing like seeing the documents to see how much trouble America is in [in] Afghanistan. America cannot conduct special operations like that and cannot win a war that way." He believes the US and its allies should pull out of Afghanistan as fast as possible.

In June 2010, a United Nations investigator called for a halt to CIA-directed drone strikes on suspected Islamic militants in Pakistan and Afghanistan, warning that killings ordered far from the battlefield could lead to a video-game mentality. The extrajudicial executions by missile strikes are justified by the Americans when it is impossible to capture insurgents alive. America is believed to control its fleet of drones from CIA headquarters in Virginia, where it coordinates the air strikes with the help of civilian pilots located near hidden airfields in Afghanistan and Pakistan who fly the drones remotely. Because operators are based thousands of kilometres away from the battlefield and undertake operations entirely through computer screens, these pilots develop a video-game mentality toward killing.

The CIA's use of unmanned Predator or Reaper drones in Afghanistan and Pakistan against Al-Qaeda and Taliban suspects have led to the deaths of thousands of innocent civilians. This is one way in which the CIA is accountable to nobody, not even to Congress. It should have no place in a civilised world, where it is licensed to kill people and act as judge, jury, and executioner. All the CIA's killings are illegal and will encourage many other countries to develop the technology that will become a major threat to world peace. It won't be long before many other rogue countries will develop guided missiles and drones of their own and will be ready to use them against their enemies or sell them to other enemies of America and Israel.

The joint military commando unit in the Afghanistan war was called Task Force 373. The CIA was part of the Task Force. Its agents' participation in the unit is a good example of their brutal activities when they are dispatched to capture or kill high-value targets, which they do by dropping bombs on them, firing Hellfire missiles, or just shooting them. Unfortunately, they often hit the wrong person. Their history is littered with destroying the wrong building and killing the wrong people while their original target is still alive and well.

The Task Force was originally established as Task Force 20 following the invasion of Iraq and then became Task Force 171 when it was moved to Afghanistan. It later became Task Force 373. Its number could swell to become Task Force 373000 or maybe higher when it kills that many innocent people, including women and children.

The CIA failures can be illustrated in a typical leaked war log of details of one of their deadly missions on June 17, 2007, to kill a Libyan senior Al-Qaeda fighter in Afghanistan, Abu Laith al-Libi. The unit was armed with a new weapon, known as Himars (high mobility artillery rocket system; a pod of six missiles on the back of a small truck). The plan was to launch five rockets at targets in the village of Nangar Khel, where TF 373 believed Libi was hiding and then to send in ground troops. The result was that they failed to find Libi but they thought they had killed six Taliban fighters. Then, when they approached the rubble of a madrasa (school), they found they had killed seven non-combatants, all of them children.

It is worth noting that Abu Laith al-Libi was reported to have been killed in a different attack in North Waziristan, Pakistan, on January 29, 2008.

Another revelation reported by the *Washington Post* is that a group of US soldiers faced the accusation of randomly targeting and killing Afghan civilian for *sport*. The reported incidents were from the army's legal documents and interviews with soldiers of a platoon from the 5th Stryker Combat Brigade, 2nd Infantry Division, who were involved in the case. According to the report, the soldiers' game started when an Afghani man approached a US soldier in the village of La Mohammed Kalay. One soldier created the impression that he and his men were under attack and followed up by tossing a fragmentary grenade on the ground. This prompted the other soldiers to open fire, killing the man. Members of the platoon have also been charged with dismembering and photographing corpses, as well as hoarding a skull and other human bones. These unprovoked attacks were the start of a month-long shooting spree against civilians that resulted in some of the grisliest allegations against American soldiers since the US invasion of Afghanistan in 2001. Army officials have not disclosed a motive for the killings, but a review of military court documents and interviews with people familiar with the investigation suggest that the killings were committed essentially for sport by soldiers who had a fondness for hashish and alcohol.

The WikiLeaks Iraq's War files and Afghan War diary show the extent of atrocities committed against civilians. The files are published online by the *Guardian*, the *New York Times* and Germany's *Der Spiegel* and includes details many incidents in which coalition forces have killed civilians. The

Guardian says the leaks show that troops killed hundreds of civilians in previously unreported incidents. Overall, these documents amount to a real-time history of the war reported from an important vantage point of the soldiers and officers actually doing the fighting and reconstruction. These documents bring the truth to light and expose America and its allies committing atrocities against a civilian population in the name of fighting terrorism.

To silence their critics, the chairman of the Joint Chief of Staff, Admiral Mike Mullen unleashed the FBI to investigate the whistleblower and waged an attack on the founder of WikiLeaks, Julian Assange. It is their way of shooting the messenger, instead of changing their behaviour and acting as humans towards their fellows humans. Assange rightfully has defended the release and said, "The documents show the true nature of the Afghan conflict." He added, "So all these people were killed in the small events that we haven't heard about which numerically eclipse the big events. It's the boy killed by a shell that missed the target. It's villagers that have gone to hospital as a result of a missed air strike."

(Thanks to you, Julian Assange. You are publishing in the public interest. You are not like some journalists who are embedded with the troops and who are unable to tell the whole story. The military will always try to make sure that their atrocities and the killing of innocent civilians are kept secret.)

It is ironic that if the American government had not been subjected to critical media coverage of the war in

Vietnam and Americans' outrage at the atrocities being committed there, the chances are the fighting and the killings would've continued to this day. It is also ironic that many World War II criminals were prosecuted for lesser crimes.

America doesn't seem to understand that the horrible act of killing women and children in an aimless war can only result in resentment and revenge. When someone bombs your wedding or shoots your kids, it is certain and natural to have feelings of revenge and retaliation. In the process of killing innocent civilians, covering it up, and pretending to be the good guys, the American military are insulting the intelligence of the whole world. Worse yet, people of the world are now fully conscious of the fact that American atrocities in the name of the "war on terror" have actually increased terrorism.

Often, people listen to apologies from US and NATO commanders about the many publicised civilian casualties when there are many more unpublicised atrocities against civilians that are swept under the carpet and lied about to avoid the sensitivity of the issue in Pakistan and Afghanistan. Andrew Bird, a media adviser who served in Afghanistan and earlier in Iraq, has revealed that a culture of excessive spin and unnecessary secrecy stopped important information reaching the public. Bird, who subsequently left the army as an information operations and media adviser, said, "The defense force deliberately obscured or painted an overly rosy picture of the war in places like Afghanistan. The way that we communicated is all government-centric. It just relayed the government's message. Every picture we have taken with every vision we presented and every interview we did, was to support the government's view."

All the spin and the lies, however, will not result in the defeat of the Taliban. Also, putting an "Afghan face" on this war by recruiting and training Afghan soldiers is difficult when members of the various ethnic groups that make up Afghanistan recruits are deeply divided. For these recruits, the problem is not just the terror of facing death at the hands of the Taliban but the burden of regimentation and the shock of serving alongside infidels. Many of these recruits will see the benefit of joining the Taliban and will abandon America's unworthy puppet government. These facts are now well recognised by the US and NATO forces, as behind-the-scenes talks with the Taliban have begun. The most likely outcome will be to allow the Taliban to govern on condition that they isolate Al-Qaeda from the region. (This is a strange American face-saving excuse for their exit or stay strategy.)

There is a divergence in agendas, regionally and globally, which could result in further isolation of America, as America prefers the "fight-now-and-talk-later" strategy, but the Afghan government, Britain, and the United Nations all prefer to negotiate and bring the war to a speedy conclusion. America's aforementioned strategy is influenced by its generals, who for the sake of saving face usually ask for more resources and surges to win but unfortunately, always end up losing. How can they win with their lack of understanding of Afghanistan's political and social environment? They can't win if they are easily fooled by the Taliban, as was demonstrated by their dealings with an impersonator of a prominent Taliban leader, Mullah Akhtar Mohammad Mansour, thinking that he could be the one who would bring the war to an end. The fake Taliban member was paid thousands of dollars by the Americans and the British for his role in secret Afghan peace negotiations. The imposter was flown by MI6 on British military planes to many meetings with the Afghan government in the belief that he could help bring peace to the country.

The Agency Coordinating Body for Afghan Relief (ACBAR) representing aid groups in Afghanistan said, "The strategy of seeking a military victory is not going to work. Sending more troops into Afghanistan would make the situation even worse. It may be that the sooner the troops withdraw, the better it will be for the people of Afghanistan."

It is worth noting that ACBAR has been working with the people of Afghanistan since 1988 and represents more than 100 local and international non-government groups, including World Vision, Save the Children, and Care International.

To stop the deterioration of the situation and the desperation of the Afghan people, the Taliban should be brought back and the American manufactured democracy abandoned. Afghanistan and indeed all other countries would be better off left alone. With or without military intervention, Afghanistan, in few decades will be stable and ready to move forward in a normal way. Removing foreign troops from the region could also save Pakistan from total disintegration.

The war on terror is not going to end with the war in Afghanistan and Pakistan; it will spread into many other Islamic countries where the decentralised Al-Qaeda has established or will establish roots, especially in countries like Egypt, Sudan, Algeria, Mauritania, Iraq, Somalia, Yemen, Jordan, and Morocco. (See below sub-heading: Turmoil in the Middle East and North Africa.)

It is not surprising to see many countries, such as Britain, France and Germany now favouring the inclusion of the Taliban in the Afghan government as part of an exit strategy for ending the war, because they came to the conclusion that first, the Taliban are too powerful to defeat and are more suited to Afghanistan's political and social environment. Training and equipping the Afghan army can only result in civil war after foreign forces leave the country. Civil war in Afghanistan will engulf its neighbouring countries, especially India and Pakistan, each of which is armed with nuclear weapons. Second, terrorism is getting worse and spreading to other counties, which is becoming detrimental to world security.

The Afghan adventure hasn't worked. The world is now more vulnerable to terrorism because the war was implemented hastily and then interrupted for an illegal war in Iraq. How many more soldiers and civilians have to die before people wake up and see that wars are outdated and that wasted lives leave permanent psychological scars?

Hopefully, America and it allies now understand that the best source for Al-Qaeda's recruitment is American and allied killings of Muslims in occupied Islamic countries. Furthermore, America and Israel need to understand that wars lead to destruction, injustice, corruption, and poverty and that a reaction to war is resentment and revolt.

Aggressive and extremist politicians, before engaging troops, should pause and think, **"There must be a better way."**

Turmoil in the Middle East and North Africa

The ripples and convulsion in the region will continue to spread relative to poverty, unemployment, food inflation, and high energy cost. It is further aggravated by the entrenchment of tribalism and religion, lack of education, dictatorships and corruption. The economical, religious, political and social problems brought the unrest to a boiling point.

While a huge gap exists between the corrupt rich of the ruling elites and the poor, coupled with stagnated economies, the turmoil will continue for many years to come. High unemployment, food inflation and high energy cost, where the majority of people living on $2 a day will ensure the upheaval get worse.

The genesis of the crisis has its roots in the twentieth century when the Western world's preoccupation was with getting cheap oil supply and looting the riches of the Arab world. In the process they were ignoring the social and cultural development of the region, at the same time of implementing a "divide and conquer" policy. As a result, the West is now witnessing an upheaval of an enormous potential. The popular revolutions that started in Tunisia are most likely will take a religious direction. However, the outcome of most of these revolutions will depend on the army's' role in each of the troubled countries. Historically, when anarchy and riot took place, the military often used the opportunity to step in and establish military dictatorship as an excuse for maintaining law and order and saving the country. They dismiss the government and abolished the country's constitution and become the absolute rulers, with prompting and backing of Western powers.

After many decades of ruling by military and monarchical dictatorships, a huge political vacuum is created, which makes the emergence of a well-structured secular democracies extremely difficult. Secular political parties and groups cannot match the power and influence of existing religious groups and parties. Religious establishments own and control the infrastructure of mosques and Islamic schools, which enable them to dictate the political message, especially under the most powerful and emotive Islamic banner of "God is Great", in Arabic, "Allah U Akbar."

Therefore, Islamist religious leaders will eventually become the rulers and dictators of the future Arab world, if the militaries decide to stay on the sideline. The Western world in the meantime should plan for the worst, as the secular middle class and other disenfranchised people will not be ready to counter the power of entrenched Islam. The first pillar of democracy is the separation of religion and state, which the Arab world is far from ready for, mainly because of the absence of effective secular political leaders. The vacuum is created by America, France and Britain when they were actively plotting to eliminate many of the secular leaders of the 1950s, 1960s and 1970s, like Gamal Abdel Nasser of Egypt, Abdul Karim Qasim of Iraq, Hafez al Assad of Syria, Ahmed Ben Bella of Algeria and Mohammad Mussadaq of Iran. Since then, they prevented any secular nationalistic leader to emerge.

It should now be expected that some Arab countries will emerge as moderate Islamists, others will be hardliners and the rest will turn into failed states. Failed states where ethnic and tribal social structure is dominant, like Yemen, Libya, Algeria, Sudan and Iraq are most likely to be influenced by Al-Qaeda or other jihadist groups. However, if the West and Israel adopt an aggressive approach in the new paradigm, most of Arab countries could end up as hardline Islamists or failed states. America and Israel have a choice between the Muslim Brotherhood style of Islamic regimes or failed states. Rejecting Muslim Brotherhood's style regime will make America and Israel very vulnerable, not only in the region, but around the world.

Muslim Brotherhood regime is a better option to live with than failed states under the influence of Al-Qaeda.

If America wants to avoid the unintended consequences, it must abandon its approach of installing corrupt regimes to serve its strategic interests. Hopefully, America has by now learnt from its experience in Iraq and Afghanistan that installing a fake and corrupt democracy or a democracy under the point of a gun has no place in the modern world and simply no longer works. Installing regimes that people may fear will sooner or later have the roles reversed, especially when unemployment and poverty set-in and the boiling point is reached. In any country, creating forty percent youth unemployment, while the autocratic rulers enjoy obscene luxuries is inhumane and a recipe for revolt.

Given a chance of harmonious coexistence with the West and in a spirit of cooperation, moderate Islamic regime can become democratic, even in the absence of Western values.

America and its allies should now expect that the Middle East and North Africa will be in state of flux for many years to come and their wrong policies can cause catastrophic results. Hopefully, America and its allies have by now learnt that planning for long-term gains from a harmonious world is better than short-term military advantage.

Hopelessness and desperation making people react violently against whomever they feel is the cause of their predicament. Entrenched poverty and high unemployment, combined with religious fundamentalism are turning Islamic countries into breeding and recruitment grounds for a decentralised Al-Qaeda and other jihadist groups. America and its allies are indirectly enhancing Osama bin Laden's image as a cult figure, which is causing the decentralisation of Al-Qaeda and the emergence of more Muslim fanatics to form more independent cells to fight for a religious cause. The entrenchment and decentralisation of Al-Qaeda is also due to many Arab leaders being compliant with Israel and America's policies against the Palestinians and even their own people, which is causing the Islamic fanatical tide to grow and threaten the survival of the West's puppet regimes.

The dangers are now fomenting a new wave of terrorism that could include bio-terrorism and dirty bombs. Unfortunately, it is not a matter of *if*; it is a matter of *when*.

Pakistan on the Brink

The expansion of war on terror from Afghanistan into Pakistan will sooner or later bring Pakistan to the brink. Its fragile economy can only exist on foreign aid and its democracy, corrupted by social division between the rich and the poor, is unsustainable. It is further aggravated by the division between secular and fanatical Muslims. The entrenchment of Al-Qaeda and the Taliban in the country is not accidental; it has its root in the country's Islamic education system that entrenches deep indoctrination and intolerance of other religions. The country is politically fractured, economically destitute with high unemployment, and militarily challenged. If it is not already a failed state, it is heading rapidly towards pariah status and could become an international outcast. It is also rapidly heading towards a civil war in addition to its struggle and constant high tension with its nuclear neighbour, India.

Pakistan is a country under siege from its increasingly assertive militant opposition groups. The militants' attacks are a direct consequence of America's war on terrorism that turned Pakistan into both a victim and a protagonist in the conflict in Afghanistan. Its western and northern fringes are devastated by America's driven counter-insurgency campaign and its heartlands are wrecked by growing violence. The country shows every sign of slipping out of control with a dysfunctional civilian government and military that has held it together for many years.

Furthermore, India has a direct interest in the outcome of a weakened nuclear Pakistan. Any future conflict between them will spell the end of America's puppet government in Afghanistan. Chronic insecurity, political civil war, intensifying economic woes, recent flooding, entrenched poverty, high unemployment, and lack of education are compounding the sense that the country is isolated, weak, and in danger of imploding.

Heightened tensions with India, friction with Afghanistan, China's rising alarm over its neighbour's predicament, and international worries about the safety of Pakistan's nuclear weapons stockpile should be the biggest worry for the world. Unfortunately, America's current main focus is to defeat the Taliban and Al-Qaeda, rather than worrying about the consequences of Pakistan's collapse. America is also ignoring another enemy; the jihadist organisation Lashkar-e-Taiba, whose main objective is to undermine the Pakistani government during the political crisis by trying to create a vacuum of power in which eventually the jihadists can take over. The creation of internal chaos is the aim of all jihadists in the country; they are being aided and abetted by Pakistan's mainstream politicians.

The vicious in-fighting between Asif Ali Zardari's Pakistan's People Party (PPP) and Nawaz Sharif's Pakistan Muslim League (PML) is similar to the earlier battles between Sharif and president Zardari's murdered wife, Benazir Bhutto, which led directly to Musharraf's military coup.

Zardari took control of the PPP after the assassination of Benazir Bhutto in 2007. He became president a year later but has been dogged by allegations of corruption. Many of Pakistan's politicians who are wealthy hereditary landlords are similarly accused of corruption.

The battle will eventually culminate in the religious jihadists backed by the Jamaat-e-Islami Pakistan group taking control of the country, with or without the help of Pakistan's Muslim League. Unfortunately, the situation is badly aggravated by America's pressure on Pakistan's government to widen the attack on Pakistani Taliban groups, in addition to its own cross-border attacks using Predator drones armed with missiles, which is alienating tribal leaders and encouraging their radicalisation. Additionally, the attacks are uniting three partisan factions with a long history of feuding, which will make America's and Pakistan's task much harder. As reported in the *New York Times* in December 2010, these factions are: Quetta Shura Taliban of Mullah Muhammad Omar, the Haqqani family, and fighters loyal to the Hekmatyar clan.

Pakistan's disintegration is a tragedy of far-reaching dimensions and poses the biggest threat to the security of the world. It is a tragedy which, on its present course, no one in the world can stop; a tragedy caused by America's aggression and lack of wisdom.

The collapse of Pakistan will reverberate throughout the rest of the Islamic world with major implications, as described in my earlier book entitled *Thorny Opinion*.

Worse of all, Pakistan's nuclear stockpile is facing a greater threat from Islamic extremists than any other nuclear stockpile on earth. Pakistan is resisting calls for it to pull back its weapons program, including its plans for expanded production of weapons-grade fuel, but insists that its small but growing arsenal is well guarded. Pakistan's reassurance is the opposite of what is stated in a report in the April 2010, issue of *Securing the Bomb*, published by the Belfer Centre for Science and International Affairs at Harvard University. The report warned of the very real possibility that nuclear warheads could be stolen by Islamic extremists. The Harvard study cited Pakistan as the country most vulnerable to this kind of attack from both the inside and the outside. Despite extensive security measures, there is a very real possibility that sympathetic insiders might carry out or assist in a nuclear theft or assist a sophisticated outsider attack, possibly with inside help to overwhelm the defences. It should not be forgotten that Pakistan's own secret service has dubious loyalty; some of its elements are more sympathetic to the Taliban than to the government.

On his visit to India in July 2010, British Prime Minister David Cameron warned Pakistan it would face international isolation if it continues to export terrorism and support extremist groups. Mr. Cameron accused Pakistan of "looking both ways," publicly condemning the Taliban while secretly supporting Afghan militants. This rhetoric is a reflection of the West's lack of understanding that Pakistan has no choice. When America decides that the war in Afghanistan cannot be won and opts for pulling out its forces, Pakistan will be left to cope and live with the Taliban forces and other jihadists. Its posture is an insurance policy that will allow it to avoid a major civil war by dealing with the Taliban while pretending to fighting them. Adding to this is the West's encouragement of India to further develop its nuclear industry and eventually its nuclear military arsenal, which poses the biggest threat to Pakistan's survival. This can be seen in the British government's shift in its nuclear policy towards India in approving the export of civil nuclear technology, which brings it in line with America's decision in 2008 that allowed India access to global nuclear commerce, despite the fact that India not being a nuclear treaty signatory.

Pakistan is thought to have between seventy and ninety nuclear warheads, but insists that its program is made necessary by neighbouring India's nuclear buildup and access to US technology for its nuclear power plants.

The incentive for Al-Qaeda and rogue countries to obtain dirty bombs has been created by America's attitude towards some Islamic countries and by allowing Israel to have the nuclear bomb with impunity and without considering the implications. It's known fact that Israel's bomb is aimed at its Arab and Islamic neighbours.

Terrorists with nuclear weapons: A small bomb detonated in San Francisco could kill 200,000 people. The terrorists would then claim they had more bombs ready to explode in other US cities and in London, potentially provoking widespread panic and major economic disruption. On short notice, America and the rest of the world would be in real terror.

Barack Obama remarked at the 2010 nuclear proliferation summit that nuclear material the size of an apple would be enough to kill thousands of people if it fell into the hands of terrorists. If terrorists got their hands on a nuclear weapon it would be a catastrophe for the world. Terrorist networks such as Al-Qaeda have tried to acquire the material for a nuclear weapon and if they ever succeed, they will surely build the bomb and use it.

Dr. Francis Slakey of Georgetown University in Washington, DC, says a revolutionary uranium enrichment process using lasers has the potential to make it much easier for rogue countries or terrorist organisations to conceal any nuclear program. "SILEX," the process of separating isotopes by laser excitation, is a new way of enriching uranium using pulsed lasers. Dr. Slakey is worried about the threat SILEX poses to global nuclear security; laser enrichment is dangerous because it is almost undetectable. It is 75 percent smaller in size than current enrichment technologies, drawing no more electricity than a dozen homes. The technology is so efficient (and so small) that satellites would not be able to detect whether there was some power source going into it, because it uses so little power. However, every past enrichment technology has proliferated despite the best efforts to keep the secret. Proliferation of this technology will most likely be pursued by rogue countries and terrorists.

Based on satellite images, the Institute for Science and International Security, the Washington nuclear watchdog, claims that a completed row of cooling towers at Pakistan's secret Khushab-III reactor indicates that the plant will soon allow Pakistan to increase its stockpile of weapons-grade plutonium. The plutonium produced at the plant allows for the construction of small but powerful weapons. Pakistan says its nuclear weapons program is necessary to counter its historic adversary India, which has a superior nuclear arsenal and conventional forces. However, in a recent report published by the *Bulletin of Atomic Scientists,* it was estimated that Pakistan had assembled seventy to ninety nuclear warheads to India's sixty to eighty, and had enough fissile material to manufacture a further ninety.

It is a pity that the Israel lobby groups who are advocating a war on Iran don't see the peril of diverting America's attention away from the forthcoming collapse of a nuclear Pakistan. The Israel lobby groups don't seem to realise that a nuclear Pakistan is the biggest threat to world security for its potential to unleash an unstoppable catastrophe.

Currently, Pakistan is surviving on American handouts when America is borrowing and printing money to sustain its own economy and fighting its unwinnable wars on many fronts. Abandoning Afghanistan and Pakistan for a war on Iran to satisfy AIPAC, as they did in Iraq, is extreme madness. It appears that the Israel lobby groups don't seem to realise that the Pakistanis are helping the Taliban and Al-Qaeda as an insurance policy against the day when America loses the will to fight and decides to pull its forces out of the region. They don't seem to realise that Pakistan has been secretly accelerating the pace of its nuclear weapons program. The Jewish religious nationalists don't want the world to have a breathing space.

The Israel lobby groups and Senator Lieberman who appears to be a leading advocate for a war on Iran should take notice of what the US State Department's counter-terrorism coordinator is reporting: that the Taliban and Al-Qaeda's core in Pakistan is the most formidable terrorist group threatening America while they are protected by the Pakistani ISI intelligence service. According to the State Department's report, Al-Qaeda, from its safe haven in Pakistan, is helping to train and fund the Taliban-led insurgency in Afghanistan, which remains resilient and is expanding. In Afghanistan, despite some heavy losses among militants and their leaders, the Taliban's ability to recruit foot soldiers from its core base of loyal rural Pashtuns has remained undiminished.

The trouble with Pakistan is that its record concerning its tolerance and complicity with terrorism and all kinds of manipulation has been so bad, and this is now confirmed in the WikiLeaks published documents. The question is, what can the world do to prevent the collapse of a crucial Islamic state that has a nuclear arsenal? There is little that America, with its "fight-now-talk-later" policy can do within a timeframe that might halt the collapse of all that remains of the Pakistani state to prevent chaos in the region. Except however, if America decides to declare peace with the Islamic world, treats Muslims with dignity, and insists on establishing a viable Palestinian state, with or without the help of AIPAC.

America is currently engaged in a covert war inside Pakistan without either side acknowledging the fact. While the Pakistan government is hiding the fact, so as not to provoke public anger, the Americans are aggravating the situation with their Predator drones, inadvertently killing Pakistanis loyal to the government. Adding to Pakistan's woes is the American pressure on it to conduct a major military offensive in North Waziristan against the Haqqani Network, the allies of Al-Qaeda. This is at the time when the Pakistani military is stretched too thin and even had to withdraw 70,000 troops from the borders to deal with the recent severe flooding. The American pressure is highlighted by General David Petraeus saying to the Pakistanis, "Either you do this, or we will do it," which means that America is frustrated with Pakistan's lack of action against the Taliban and is unilaterally ready to extend the war into Pakistan. Widening the war in Pakistan, means America will be fighting not only the Taliban, but the Pakistani army as well, and by then Iran will have a formidable nuclear arsenal. America is playing with fire. **Please wake up!**

In the meantime, America is shoveling billions of dollars toward Pakistan in the belief that the Pakistani government is capable of preventing its nuclear stockpile from falling into the hands of Islamic fanatics. At the same time, the Pakistan government is to continue to allow American forces to bomb suspected Islamist militants in its territories. Unfortunately, these attacks are causing more civilian than militant casualties and resulting in more hatred towards America and its puppet government in Pakistan. Worse still, some of the helicopter and drone attacks are mistakenly hitting Pakistani soldiers who are fighting the Taliban, which is provoking *more* resentment within the Pakistani military towards America and its allies.

Adding to Pakistan's troubles are the natural disasters it has had to deal with. The government's response to these proves that they are hopeless in coming to the rescue of their citizens. The recent earthquake in Kashmir killed more than 70,000 people, and the devastating flooding in July and August 2010 killed thousands. More than 20 million people were affected; the majority lost all their possessions and became homeless.

The flood has affected a vast area at huge economic cost, wiping out 30 percent of the cotton crop and damaging a significant proportion of food crops in the breadbasket provinces of Punjab and Sindh. Every main bridge in the Swat Valley, in the north, was destroyed and it took many months to get electricity back to the region. The loss of human lives and infrastructure was colossal, and Pakistan has no resources with which to cope with such disasters.

Furthermore, the flood has played into the hands of extremist groups who helped the affected people in the absence of the government's ability to do so. Worse still, according to officials at the National Disaster Management Authority, the Pakistan Peoples Party leaders exerted political pressure to ensure their constituencies were given priority in aid distribution of food and medicine at the expense of others.

Until January 2011, the flood still covered many parts of Pakistan and affected over two million people—people who live in absolute poverty. The catastrophe has proved that Pakistan is an unviable state both politically and economically and that its collapse will culminate in rioting and chaos unless America is prepared to spend a trillion dollars to rebuild Pakistan and to keep propping up a bankrupt nation and a corrupt government. In the interim however, a military coup is the most likely outcome before the final social, political, and economic disintegration of Pakistan.

The solution for Pakistan is to allow the Taliban to govern Afghanistan to give it a breathing space in which to restructure its social, political, and economic system with the help of the Western world.

America Rethinks: America is now rethinking (probably too late) its strategies and is considering abandoning its long-held delusion that it can conduct two major conventional wars at any one time. On discovering its weakness and vulnerability, it has decided to deal with one conflict rather than all those it has planned for. In 2010,

Secretary of Defense Robert Gates said, "The old doctrine ignored reality." He added, "The U.S. engagement in two wars has already stretched beyond the length of World War Two. We have learned through painful experience that the wars we fight are seldom the wars that we planned." He further said, "The need was to re-balance the military to be more capable of handling today's conflicts—Iraq, Afghanistan, Al-Qaeda and its allies—and challenges such as cyber-terrorism and nuclear proliferation."

His comments confirming the rethinking in the US defence doctrine came as America's top intelligence official told legislators that he was highly certain that Al-Qaeda or one of its affiliates would attempt a large-scale attack on US soil soon.

Gates conclusion was, "The U.S. needed to balance resources and risk according to four key objectives. The first imperative was to prevail in today's wars; the second, to prevent and deter conflicts; the third, to prepare the military for a wide range of contingencies; and, finally, to preserve and enhance America's all-volunteer force. As a result, the United States needs a broad portfolio of military capabilities with maximum versatility across the widest possible spectrum of conflict."

In his book *Obama's War*, Bob Woodward, associate editor of the *Washington Post,* revealed that Barack Obama wanted his top military advisers to present him with an exit plan from Afghanistan, which he never got. Frustrated with his military commanders for offering only options that required significantly more troops, the president crafted his own strategy, dictating a classified "terms sheet" that sought to limit US involvement without talking of victory as an objective. "This needs to be a plan about how we're going to hand it off and get out of Afghanistan," Mr. Obama is quoted as telling aides as he laid out his reasons for adding 30,000 personnel in a short-term escalation. "I'm not doing ten years," he told the Secretary of Defense Robert Gates and Secretary of State Hillary Clinton at a meeting on October 26, 2009. "I'm not doing long-term nation building. I am not spending a trillion dollars."

The book also focuses on the strategy review and the dissension, distrust, and infighting that consumed the national security team as it was locked in a fierce and emotional struggle over the direction, goals, timetable, troop levels, and chances of success for a war that is almost certain to be one of the defining events of Obama's presidency. Obama's preference is for reconciliation with the Taliban.

It is worth noting that Woodward also quotes the commander in Afghanistan, Gen. David Petraeus, as saying "The war in Afghanistan is unwinnable, but the US should keep fighting." He also said, "This is the kind of fight we're in for the rest of our lives and probably our kid's lives." And he was further quoted describing the Afghan government as a "criminal syndicate protected by US power." **Wow!**

It is ironic that despite the analyses and conclusions, America is still bogged down with wars on many fronts and more will be added if it goes along with Israel's demand for a new war on Iran and Syria, based on the pretence that Iran will soon have the nuclear bomb and Syria is arming Hezbollah with scud missiles.

In recent developments, the Obama administration endorsed the Afghan efforts to negotiate peace with the Taliban, which means it is backing off from its earlier stance that there would be no talk with the Taliban until the war is all but won. The new acceptance of reconciliation is seen as an admission that the war is going badly. Publicising US support for any peace talks is also seen as a sign that the administration is looking for ways to demonstrate a commitment to ending the war, short of calling home large numbers of troops. On the other hand, the Taliban representatives insist they will not negotiate so long as foreign troops occupy their country, saying that no one who speaks for the group is in talks with the Afghan government.

To counter the Taliban, the Americans are insisting that as part of any peace deal, the insurgents must lay down their weapons, cut ties with Al-Qaeda, and pledge to respect the Afghan constitution with its protections for women's rights. **America, please stop kidding!**

War in Iraq

The war in Iraq was part of a plan for a forced regime change in any Middle Eastern country that is critical of America and Israel. To allow the economic expansion of America and the territorial expansion of Israel, it became necessary to install new regimes that are loyal and willing to serve their interests. History shows that this cannot be achieved without installing corrupt governments that operate on a basis of mutual benefit. In the process, these corrupt governments enrich themselves at the expense of impoverishing their nations. The outcome of which, is disenfranchised and desperate people reacting violently against whoever causing their plight. These people who have nothing left to lose are recruited to fight for a cause, often for religious and nationalistic causes.

Unfortunately, this is what that Iraq war has achieved, and the same outcome is expected in Afghanistan and Pakistan. The Iraq war was one of those wars that are designed to allow America to have direct control over an oil-rich country and at the same time to protect Israel and allow it to expand.

Declassified documents and documents released following a request under the Freedom of Information Act show that former president George W. Bush's advisers focused on toppling Saddam Hussein's regime as soon as he took office and discussed how to justify a war in Iraq shortly after invading Afghanistan in 2001. A few hours after the September 11 attacks in 2001, according to notes of a meeting on that day, then defense secretary Donald Rumsfeld spoke of attacking Iraq as well as Osama bin Laden. Furthermore, according to the papers posted by the Washington-based National Security Archive, an independent research institute, Rumsfeld told a Pentagon lawyer to go to his deputy to get support showing a supposed link between the Iraqi regime and Al-Qaeda's founder.

Confronting Iraq was also the focus of a July 2001 memo to the national security adviser at the time, Condoleezza

Rice, with Rumsfeld urging a high-level meeting on policy towards Baghdad. Forecasting an optimistic outcome far from the result the Iraq war actually produced, Rumsfeld said that Washington's image in the region and the world would benefit from toppling Saddam. Another document shows Rumsfeld discussing war plans for Iraq just two months after the 2001 US invasion of Afghanistan. In a meeting with then head of US Central Command General Tommy Franks, Rumsfeld told him to ready forces for the decapitation of the Iraqi regime.

The rest is history. Saddam's regime was decapitated and the horror of Islamic backlash and radicalisation was under way. Following its "shock and awe" slogan, America pursued the delusion of winning the war with Bush's premature declaration, "Mission accomplished."

The Iraq war is anything but "won," if that means reducing violence to a level where society can function without bombings or large-scale incidents of violence or the risk of new outbreaks of major ethnic and sectarian violence. Much of the violence in Iraq has an ethnic and sectarian character, entrenched by America's designed Iraqi constitution that is aimed at dividing Iraqis along ethnic and sectarian lines—a division that makes national security impossible to achieve. Sunni activists, together with the previous Baathist regime, see Iran orchestrating the political environment in the country. The Iranian intervention and the American manipulation provoke a feeling of conspiracy within the Sunni population. Adding fuel to the fire is America's signal of support to the Kurds to take control of Kirkuk, where large oil reserves exist. A coalition of Shiites and Kurds has left Sunnis in a weaker position. Because of the disenfranchisement of Sunnis and the feeling of an American conspiracy, the stage is set for an everlasting sectarian conflict and concomitant hatred towards America, which will make Iraq an ungovernable state for many years to come. Iraq's constitution, written by the Americans, has sown the seeds for permanent social and political division, which will backfire on its creator.

The world will witness Iraq as a state which resembles Lebanon and Nigeria combined. Lebanon's similarity is reflected in its sectarian constitution, which is a source of constant conflict and civil wars. Nigeria is similarly reflected in the constant blowing-up of oil pipelines because of the disenfranchisement of segments of the population.

In his book *The Gamble: General Petraes and the American Military Adventure in Iraq,* reporter for military affairs for the *Washington Post* Thomas Ricks focuses on the military surge in Iraq and what lies beyond it for the Obama administration. He warns that the gains of the surge could easily unravel and that the administration will face some very tough choices, including a confrontation with the generals. The generals believe that there is no such thing as non-combat troops, just as there is no pacifist wing in the U.S. Army. All the troops are ready for combat. All American troops will be fighting and dying in Iraq for many years to come. He warns that this will be extremely tough.

Ricks paints a gloomy picture of the scenario in Iraq, especially for the gradual withdrawal of troops from areas that aren't so secure, that aren't so safe, and that the army is worried about. He further argues that the basic problems the surge was meant to solve have not been solved, including the friction between the Sunnis and Shiites and between the Shiites and the Kurds.

The world is currently only witnessing the occasional coordinated and suicide bombing of buildings and civilian targets, but when the Americans leave the country, the situation will be more dire and will include oil installations, bridges, and other strategic targets of destabilisation campaigns. The disenfranchisement of Sunnis is a haven for Al-Qaeda and other jihadist recruiters for the Arab and Islamist causes. The main jihadist organisations currently active in Iraq are Jaish al-Mohammad, the Salaheddin Army, and the Islamic Army of Iraq.

Sectarian war in Iraq is not far away as can be easily seen from the bitterly contested election on March 7, 2010, in which Iyad Allawi, the former and secular prime minister scored a surprise win. Consequently, the Shiite religious and theocratic parties, encouraged by Iran, united to prevent him from forming a government. Although Allawi is a Shiite, his being secular has attracted the majority of the Sunni parties to his side. The Sunnis are the most disfranchised groups and have suffered most from the American invasion of Iraq. The internal conflict in Iraq will not remain within its borders, but has the potential to spread to its neighbouring countries and reach the world at large.

Iran is playing a major role in uniting the pro-Tehran factions for the control of the Iraqi government under its preferred prime minster, Nouri al-Maliki. The deal not only involves Iraqi Shiites, but Syria and the Lebanese group Hezbollah. Iran's idea is to create a buffer to counter

America's interests, especially as America is in the process of changing its relationship with Iraq from military occupier to civilian partner. Analysts say that Iran's activities behind the scenes began to intensify as soon as America decided to withdraw its combat troops from Iraq.

Iran's move to control the political agenda in Iraq will be the recipe for endless conflict not only in Iraq but throughout the Middle East. The signs of what lies ahead can be seen in the WikiLeaks diplomatic cables published in November 2010. In one of the documents, King Abdullah of Saudi Arabia urged the United States to attack Iran to destroy its nuclear program and to "cut off the head of the snake."

But for Iraq, there is no government capable at this stage to serve either American or Iranian interests, despite the fact that America occupies Iraq while Iran is gaining control of Iraq at many levels of the Iraqi government. The disenfranchising of the Sunnis will sooner or later culminate in an all-out civil war.

America and Britain Have Failed Iraq and the World

American and Britain have failed Iraq, as can be seen from the original British and American conspiracy detailed by the former chief of British Secret Intelligence Service (SIS) Sir John Scarlett in his dossier of 2002 that persuaded the British Parliament to support the case for war. In his testimony to the Chilcot inquiry, he said that then Prime Minister Tony Blair had received two secret intelligence reports that made it clear that Saddam Hussein did not have weapons of mass destruction. These were delivered in the weeks leading up to the invasion of Iraq. He said the British intelligence service had received one report just thirteen days before the invasion which stated clearly that Saddam had no missiles that could reach Israel or were capable of carrying biological or chemical weapons. Scarlett, who headed the Joint Intelligence Committee between 2001 and 2004, also distanced himself from Blair's earlier claims that intelligence had established beyond doubt that Iraq possessed weapons of mass destruction.

In another testimony from Tony Blair's former colleague and a cabinet minister, Clare Short presented evidence showing that Blair was running a dishonest and dysfunctional government that played to the Americans at a time of war. She said, "I don't remember, at all, Iraq coming to the cabinet in any way whatsoever, at that time." She also said that she was taken aback when Attorney-General Lord Goldsmith "appeared at a cabinet meeting with new advice, saying he firmly believed an invasion was legal, only days before the war began." She added, "I said, well that's extraordinary, why is it so late? Did you change your mind?" And they all said, 'Clare, stop.' Everything was very fraught by then and they didn't want me arguing, and I was jeered at to be quiet. That's what happened." She added, "If he won't answer, and then the prime minister's saying, be quiet and that's it, no discussion, there's only so much you can do."

But perhaps Ms. Short's most damning evidence came in reaction to Mr. Blair's earlier assertion that after the September 11 attacks, the rules had changed forever. She said, "Tony Blair's account of the need to act urgently somehow because of September 11, I think doesn't stack up to any scrutiny whatsoever." She added, "We've made Iraq more dangerous as well as causing enormous suffering."

Since these testimonies, in January 2011, Tony Blair has come under pressure ahead of his second appearance at the Iraq war inquiry, after the former attorney-general revealed Blair's public comments ahead of the 2003 Iraq invasion contradicted his legal advice. In a written statement to the Chilcot inquiry, Lord Goldsmith revealed he was "uncomfortable" about Blair's public comments that Britain could attack Iraq without further United Nations backing when he was receiving clear legal advice to the contrary. Goldsmith's statement suggested Blair may have misled Parliament over the legality of the war. Goldsmith said he advised Blair on January 14, 2003 that a UN Security Council resolution on Iraq was not enough on its own to justify force against Iraq, but the following day Blair told members of Parliament that while a second UN resolution was "preferable," there were circumstances in which it was "not necessary," that is, in the event of the use of an "unreasonable veto" by a Security Council member.

Clare Short resigned as a result of the war. She felt it may have been avoided if only the UN weapons inspectors under Hans Blix had been given more time in Iraq as there was no reason to rush, except that the Americans wanted the invasion.

It is worth noting that Hans Blix, the United Nations chief weapons inspector, has testified at the Chilcot inquiry. He criticised both the British and American governments over their role in the run-up to the Iraq war. His team of inspectors had visited 500 sites but found no evidence of weapons of mass destruction. He told the inquiry that it was curious that the US and Britain were saying further inspections were useless when he was upbeat about Iraqi cooperation.

This is in addition to the warning to Tony Blair by the former head of Britain's intelligence service (MI5) that there was no intelligence to justify the war in Iraq and the war would substantially increase the terrorist threat to the UK, whilst Saddam Hussein posed no threat to Britain.

In fact, the war has resulted in more Muslims prepared to engage in terrorism. MI5 later discovered that by 2004, eighty British men were fighting in Iraq on the side of the insurgency against the coalition forces.

Under international law, attack on a sovereign state without legitimacy is a crime. The invasion of Iraq and the ensuing bloodbath is the most horrible crime of the twenty-first century. It was carried out by the so-called civilised nations of America and Britain under the disguise of ridding the world of (non-existent) weapons of mass destruction. The assault on the defenseless civilian population to give their country an unwanted democracy has resulted in the death of many innocent people. The motive for America and Britain was the control of the oil reserves of Iraq, which are the second largest in the world after Saudi Arabia. The savage multi-national companies are now in control of Iraq's resources and their next target is Iran—but for how long and will they succeed in Iran?

The movie *Avatar*, directed by James Cameron, is a cinematic illustration of the savagery of multi-national companies upon powerless countries. According to Cameron, *Avatar* implicitly criticises America's role in the Iraq War in general and the "shock and awe" element of the use of heavy weapons to destroy the country. Cameron said, "We know what it feels like to launch the missiles. We don't know what it feels like for them to land on our home soil, in America."

Controlling precious resources such as Iraq's oil is identical to the controlling of the metaphorically named "unobtanium" minerals on the film's planet Pandora. In *Avatar*, although an American corporation invades the planet in the year 2154 to extract a precious mineral by displacing the three-meter-tall blue people who live there, it's meant to be a metaphor for the invasion of Iraq. The process of destruction of the environment and the killing of thousands of the indigenous Na'vi inhabitants is similar to America's real action upon a powerless country like Iraq. It is a clear example of how much destruction they are ready to inflict on a nation to grab its essential resources.

The military commander of the invaders echoes George W. Bush as he built a rationale for invading Iraq: "Our survival relies on pre-emptive action." In *Avatar*, the invaders' description of the assault as a "shock and awe" attack is the same as the Pentagon's propaganda for its initial bombing of Baghdad.

Of the war, Cameron said, "We went down a path that cost several hundreds of thousands of Iraqi lives. I don't think the American people even know why it was done.

So it's all about opening your eyes." The movie meant to transfer the public's empathy from the invaders to the invaded.

It is to be hoped that the Americans and their British ally can now see their own side of aggression on the helpless. They launch missiles to kill people and destroy the country's infrastructure without any moral responsibility. The invasion of Iraq was much worse than that depicted in *Avatar*; the Americans are brutal and too obvious. They invade to extract the precious resource. In the Iraq invasion, the Americans were totally dishonest. Bush and Cheney's deception before invading Iraq was their claim that Saddam Hussein had a connection with Al-Qaeda and the terrorist attacks of September 11, 2001, which was refuted later—there was no collusion because Saddam Hussein was a staunch enemy of Al-Qaeda. The Bush-Cheney-Blair deception and so *Avatar* tell the people of the world to wake up.

The rise of Al-Qaeda and the anti-American feeling throughout the Arab and the Islamic worlds reached its height following the American assault on Iraq during the first Gulf War. The first Gulf War led to Osama bin Laden's outrage at Saudi Arabia, the land of Mecca, being used as a military base for US troops.

In his book *Against All Enemies: Inside America's War on Terror*, former chief counter-terrorism advisor Richard A. Clarke clearly demonstrates that George W. Bush had decided to invade Iraq long before the September 11 terrorist attack, which in effect was no more than a political marketing opportunity. Clarke's claim was supported later by Tony Blair's secret letters to Bush backing military action against Iraq the year before they ordered an invasion, as was also disclosed in January 2010 at the Chilcot inquiry.

Earlier evidence in the inquiry suggested Tony Blair decided to back Bush after they met at the president's Texas ranch in April 2002—eleven months before the British Parliament gave the go-ahead for the March 2003 invasion.

It is worth noting that following his election in September 2010 to the leadership of the British Labour Party, Ed Miliband told the party's annual conference that Labour had been wrong to back the US-led invasion of Iraq in 2003.

Another Bush-Cheney-Blair deception before invading Iraq was their claim that Saddam Hussein was hiding weapons of mass destruction, which was later debunked. The WMD was an officially sponsored lie, as demonstrated by the journalist Bob Drogin in his book *Curveball: Spies, Lies, and the Con Man Who Caused a War*. Drogin describes how CIA director George Tenet assured Secretary of State Colin Powell that their evidence was from an Iraqi defector who had worked on the WMD himself. Tenet said, "The evidence supplied by the defector, codenamed Curveball, had been corroborated by three sources." Powell repeated this claim to the world.

After the invasion, the American weapons inspector David Kay was given the responsibility to find the hidden WMD. He wanted more information from the CIA about

Curveball. "What was he like to talk to?" he asked. "Well, we've never actually talked to him," came the CIA reply. "You're kidding me, right?" Kay replied.

But it wasn't a joke. Curveball was in the hands of German intelligence. The Germans warned the CIA repeatedly that Curveball's evidence could not be verified. It turned out he was a liar, as in the years he claimed to have been working on Saddam's secret WMD, he was actually a taxi driver in Baghdad. David Kay asked the CIA about the three corroborating sources. "There really are no other sources," was the answer.

It became clearer after the invasion that the pro-invasion hawks were the Zionists and the Israel lobby groups. James Bamford, a former ABC News producer and a US intelligence expert, in his book *A Pretext for War: 9/11, Iraq, and the Abuse of America's Intelligence Agencies* gives more detail about the lies and deception employed by the Bush administration.

Patriotic Americans should revolt against the corruption of American democracy by their manipulative leaders and the subversion of their country's political and economic interests to the strategic interests of Israel. Nobody should have any doubt that Americans were manipulated into invading Iraq mainly to advance Israeli interests. This couldn't be clearer from Iraqi politician Ahmed Chalabi's statement following his secret visit to Israel in 2002 when he said, "The road to Baghdad lies through Jerusalem!" At that time, the war against Al-Qaeda in Afghanistan was effectively abandoned to invade Iraq when the pro-Israel lobby groups took advantage of the September 11 attacks to push for the invasion of Iraq to advance their interests.

Without the authorisation of the Security Council and after spending US $1 trillion, thousands of allied soldiers died, including more than 4,200 American soldiers. Millions of Iraqis became refugees and about 500,000 defenseless Iraqis died as a result of an illegal invasion of a helpless nation. The irony is that, according to US Special Forces commander Brigadier General Patrick Higgins, after eight years of war in Iraq, Al-Qaeda there remains "pretty much intact." Although Al-Qaeda in Iraq no longer appears capable of carrying out its former kind of large-scale bombings, the general thinks that the Sunni extremist organisations and other groups continue to conduct attacks almost daily.

The drawdown of American combat troops in August 2010 marks the end of a disastrous military foray that leaves Iraq vulnerable to regional terrorism, especially from Al-Qaeda and Sunni extremist forces. America thinks it has achieved the creation of a loyal government in Iraq, equipped to protect its strategic interests, but in effect it has created a government divided along ethnic and religious lines. Soon after the total American withdrawal, the nation will be ready for endless civil war that will culminate in the blowing up of oil installations and oil pipelines. 7,000 kilometers of oil pipelines in Iraq will be impossible to patrol.

America doesn't understand that the war in Iraq has just started, not ended, and that its ignorance and arrogance are the biggest threat to the world and to its own national interests.

According to a top Iraqi army officer, Lieutenant General Babker Zebari, the withdrawal of US troops will be premature, as Iraq needs the U.S. Army at least till 2020, when the Iraqi army will be ready to take control. The withdrawal of US troops will provide a new opportunity for the militants, especially in the absence of political unity, as many of the sectarian wounds that had begun to heal will be ready to reopen.

As a result of its occupation, America is leaving Iraq in a state of devastation and with a chronically corrupt government. The invasion has left Iraq not only a decimated society divided on sectarian lines but with a destroyed infrastructure and devastated middle class. The final outcome of America's war in Iraq will be **"the destruction of a nation."**

The War on Palestine

America's unconditional support of Israel and Israel's disdain towards America: Neither America nor Israel believes in justice. They apply extreme brutality against their enemies and against anything or anybody standing in their way. Their brutality is provoking resentment and revolt around the world, especially in the Islamic world. Their propaganda says: When Palestinians kill Israelis, it is terrorism, but when Israelis kill Palestinians, it is self-defence. The question to be asked is this: Is the resistance against an illegal occupation and colonisation of any country totally justified?

Israel now occupies over 42 percent of the Palestinian territories and has no intention of slowing down its colonisation of Palestine. According to human rights group B'Tselem, the growth rate of the Jewish population in the settlements in 2008 was almost three times greater than the growth rate of Israel's population, which is 5.1 percent compared with 1.8 percent.

In his book *Palestine: Peace Not Apartheid*, former president Jimmy Carter describes the Israeli forced segregation in the West Bank and the terrible oppression of the Palestinians as a violation of human decency. The book is about the occupied territories and the desire of a minority of Israelis to confiscate and colonise Palestinian land, and it is about the violation of basic human rights. This is the main cause of the conflict and Arab animosity towards Israel and America; a conflict that is threatening the whole region. He points out that, based on a Hebrew University poll, the majority of Israelis and Palestinians are in favour of a comprehensive settlement similar to the Roadmap for Peace or the Saudi proposal adopted by all Arab countries.

As president, Carter's intention was through negotiation, a land swap that could lead to a Palestinian state with defined and internationally recognised borders. This was the official US policy and was previously approved by Israeli governments in 1978 and 1993.

Unfortunately however, with the emergence of the neo-cons, supported by the evangelical fanatics and the election of a mentally weak president (George W. Bush), the whole of Middle East politics has been turned on its head. The aggressive approach towards the Middle East has resulted in an equally fanatical Islamic reaction that is still reverberating in the world today.

Israel's constant attacks on the Palestinians in the West Bank, its imprisonment or assassination of their political leaders, and its major assault on Gaza in December 2008, leaves no option for these oppressed people but to become militants. The horrific and indiscriminate killing of women and children has demonstrated that there is absolutely no symmetry or proportionality between the occupying power and the occupied people. In this instance, the resistance and the militancy against a ruthless occupying force is fully justified.

Jimmy Carter exposes Israel's rejection of the Roadmap as part of its strategy to crush Gaza and to implement its expansion plans in the West Bank. In the process, it is expecting to have the tacit cooperation of Fatah leaders by rewarding them for their capitulation.

A Nobel Peace Prize winner in 2002 for his decades of work for peace, human rights, and international development, Carter sees that Israeli sovereignty and security can co-exist permanently and peacefully alongside a Palestinian state. The lack of goodwill from the Israelis, however, results in bloody struggle, often interrupted by negotiations that turn out to be anything but honest. Carter assigns ultimate blame to Israel, arguing that the country's leadership has routinely undermined the peace process through its obstinate, aggressive, and illegal occupation of territories seized in 1967. He is decidedly less critical of

Arab leaders, accepting their concern for the Palestinian cause at face value, and including their anti-Israel rhetoric as a matter of course. He also treats the Israelis gently, considering the massive human rights abuses they have committed. This is understandable, since the Israelis have always sought America's approval before committing any major assault on the Palestinians, including the period when Jimmy Carter was the president.

Israel cannot and will not be able to carry out its aggression in the Middle East if America stands firm and says *No*. In the current atmosphere of animosity towards America, Carter's regrets should be acknowledged, as they could be a precursor for change in America's foreign policy of blind support for Israel at the expense of the Palestinians and the Arab countries; although the world should not breathe easy until America frees itself from the Israel lobby groups who control its Congress and its foreign policy. The control of the political agenda by the extreme right in both America and Israel is the stumbling block in the face of a just settlement of the conflict. Despite the fact that the moderate majority of Israelis and Palestinians are in favour of a comprehensive settlement in line with the Roadmap, the extreme right minorities are running the brutal religious nationalistic agenda.

Solving the Israeli-Palestinian problem by stopping the forced segregation and oppression of the Palestinians and colonising their land will go a long way towards solving Israel's conflict with its Arab neighbours and America's conflict with the Islamic world.

Twenty years of talk and many agreements has yielded nothing for the Palestinians but loss of more of their territories through Israel's settlements expansion. All unconditional talks constantly demanded by Israel are designed to buy more time for its further expansion. These arrogant tactics, including Israel's constant attempt to divide the Palestinians, stem from Israel's position of power that leaves no option for the Palestinians and the Islamic world but to revolt.

In his article in *Peace and Justice Post*, of July 30, 2007 entitled "Guillotining Gaza," Noam Chomsky describes the death of the Palestinian nation as a rare and somber event. The vision of a unified and independent Palestine threatens to be another casualty of a Hamas-Fatah civil war stoked by Israel and its enabling ally, the United States. In January 2006, the Palestinians voted in a carefully monitored election, pronounced free and fair by international observers. Despite US-Israeli efforts to swing the election towards their favourite, the Palestinian Authority President Mahmoud Abbas and his Fatah Party, Hamas won a surprising victory.

The punishment of Palestinians for the crime of voting the wrong way was severe. With US backing, Israel stepped up its violence in Gaza, withheld funds it was legally obligated to transmit to the Palestinian Authority, tightened its siege, and even cut off the flow of water to the arid Gaza Strip. The United States and Israel made sure that Hamas would not have a chance to govern. They rejected Hamas's call for a long-term cease-fire to allow for negotiations on a two-state settlement along the lines of an international consensus that Israel and United States have opposed. Additionally, they kept Gaza in virtual isolation.

Meanwhile, Israel stepped up its programs of annexation, assassination, imprisonment of Palestinian leaders, and dismemberment of the shrinking Palestinian cantons in the West Bank; always with US backing, despite occasional minor complaints. Additionally, Israel and the United States quickly moved to turn the outcome of Hamas control of Gaza to their benefit. They now have a pretext for tightening the stranglehold on the people of Gaza. When they can't get something by direct action, they adopt a strategy of making the Gazans' life too miserable for staying, hoping that the misery will eventually encourage them to leave the territories for a better life elsewhere. Israel is trying to achieve this by the apartheid wall, the Gaza naval blockade, the closing of all crossings, and the deprivation of the population from fuel, water, and other living essentials.

Israel and America want the Palestinians to recognise Israel and renounce violence when they themselves don't recognise Palestine as a state and don't renounce violence against the Palestinians. Even the Israeli cabinet proclaimed that the Roadmap does not compel Israel to cease violence against the Palestinians.

Bombardment of Gaza: It was reported in the Israeli press that the brutal Israeli attack on the helpless Palestinians that was launched on Gaza in December 2008 was meticulously planned. This was also highlighted in Noam Chomsky's article in *Chomsky. Info*, of June 6, 2009, entitled "Exterminate all the Brutes: Gaza 2009." In the article, Chomsky explains the narrow scope of Israeli Defence Force (IDF) logic in dealing with the Palestinians during the attack on Gaza, which was based on the interpretation of a senior figure in its international law division who said, "The people who go into a house despite a warning do not have to be taken into account in terms of injury to civilians, because they are voluntary human shields. From the legal point of view, I do not have to show consideration for them. In the case of people who return to their home in order to protect it, they are taking part in the fighting."

The Palestinians in Gaza got the message on the first day of the attack, when Israeli warplanes struck numerous targets simultaneously in the middle of a Saturday morning. Some 200 were killed instantly. Inflicting pain on civilians for political ends is another long-standing doctrine of state terror, in fact its guiding principle. The meticulous planning also presumably included the termination of the assault. It ended just before the US president's inauguration, thus minimising the (remote) threat that the newly elected President Obama might have to say some words critical of these vicious US-supported crimes.

Since America is part of Israel, or vice versa, both countries are directly or indirectly committing war crimes against a civilian population. Their crimes unfortunately cannot be punished because they are above international law.

For further discussion on Gaza, it is appropriate to highlight some paragraphs from an article *in the Sydney Morning Herald*, on January 8, 2009, by the Jewish novelist Sara Dowse, in which she wrote: "It has taken me days to begin writing this, so horrified have I been by Israel's latest actions. My sense of justice, however—as a mother, a Jew, and above all as a human being—impels me to try. The massacre in Gaza has its roots in virulent European anti-Semitism and the 1917 Balfour declaration, when the British government promised Zionists that Jewish people would have a homeland in Palestine if Britain was victorious in World War I."

It is worth noting that there was a proviso in the Balfour Declaration that giving the Jews a homeland (not a state) would not be to the detriment of the Palestinians, who were and still are the majority, when the refugees are counted. The displacement of the Palestinians and the occupation of Palestine by Jewish migrants was a consequence of World War II and the unilateral declaration by the Zionists of an Israeli state.

In the article, Dowse further wrote: "Despite the suffering of the Palestinians, whose land was taken from them, for many years the sympathy of the developed world was with Israel. The Western world assumed that Palestine as refuge for the survivors of the Nazi slaughter of European Jews, and been beleaguered by surrounding hostile Arab states. With the 1967 occupation of the West Bank and Gaza however, Israel could no longer be accepted as a victim. Yet it has continued to play on the sympathies of Western governments, most particularly on the US and on Jews of the Diasporas."

In reality, Israel has been a colonising state, masquerading as the most democratic, most humane, most modern nation in the region. It has served the Western powers to have such a proxy in the Middle East, and most recently, under the Bush Administration and in concert with the Israelis, they have played a cynical game of divide and rule, encouraging the Israelis in their blind refusal to negotiate with Hamas, just as for years Israel refused to negotiate with the Palestine Liberation Organisation (PLO), the forerunners of Fatah, whom they now support. Hamas is not a terrorist organisation, but was the legitimate, democratically elected government of the Palestinian Authority. Some people may not like what it stands for, but that is no reason for sidelining it.

In the article, under the heading *And who now would trust Israel?*, Dowse further wrote: "So here we have it; a tough, technocratically savvy, nuclear power with the backing of the largest military power the world has known, bombing, then invading, a territory the size of a small city, with a population of 1.5 million, most of whom are civilians, to defend our citizens. The ceasefire was meant to lift the Israeli blockade on Gaza, but it didn't. It was meant to facilitate the release of Palestinian prisoners, many of whom were members of the elected Hamas Government, but it didn't. Israeli planes raided southern Gaza in November. The Hamas rockets continued. Which side broke the ceasefire? Hamas may not be blameless, but the situation is far more complex than Israel claims. The fact that more than 600 people have died because in a couple of weeks the US will have a new government and next month Israel will have an election, is the most shocking form of cynicism the Palestinian people have yet faced. Since the 2006 invasion of Lebanon I have undergone what for me, as a Jew, has been an agonising realignment of my feelings about Israel. I have come to believe that a specifically Jewish state has been a terrible mistake.

A homeland is different from a state. There have been examples throughout history and there are in our own time polities with mixed ethnic populations and official sanction for their living in harmony together. Australia is one. I don't know how it will come about—I hope with as little bloodshed as possible—but I look forward to the distant day when the land becomes a multicultural country again, perhaps as a federation, perhaps in another form, but similar to what it was before it was destroyed with the poison of ethnic territorial nationalism."

As an update to the Sara Dowse article, according to the United Nations Fact Finding Mission on Gaza Conflict of September 29, 2009 report from the Hon. Judge Richard Goldstone's commission of inquiry, the actual number of people killed in Israel's raids on Gaza was 1,400 innocent people, including 320 children.

It is ironic that the collateral killing of innocent people, especially children, doesn't raise the eyebrows of the right-to-life or the pro-life movements. They are always ready to protest in front of abortion clinics to protect the rights of foetuses, but never in front of the Pentagon or the Israeli embassy against the killing of so many children. **Please wake up!**

Following the destruction of Gaza in 2008, Israel kept it under blockade. Goldstone's report called Israel's actions in Gaza "war crimes." It is worth noting that Richard Goldstone is a Jewish South African judge who became the subject of the Israeli "Get Goldstone" campaign for his criticism of Israel, despite the fact that the judge has extended his criticism to Hamas. The vicious campaign against him commenced with an article in *Yeddioth Achronoth* newspaper, in which he was accused of being a racist judge who took part in the racist policies during the Apartheid regime in South Africa. This was followed by many other articles and columns written in other newspapers, bashing Goldstone with the same accusation and was followed by a directive from the Israeli Foreign Affairs Ministry to all diplomatic missions to use the published materials in their PR presentations. In his attack, Prime Minister Benjamin Netanyahu classified the judge as a grave threat to Israel's legitimacy.

How can Israel claim legitimacy when it attacks a judge with unquestionable integrity—a man who played a crucial role in guiding South Africa through its democratic transition and transfer of power to the black majority? The role he played was embraced by Nelson Mandela, who appointed him to South Africa's highest court.

Is this another demonstration of Israel's usual method of silencing the voice of reason? Is this again a case of "who dares to speak out?"

It appears that Israel forgot its history, as the most reliable arms supplier of the Apartheid regime in South Africa, to the extent of signing a secret security pact in April 1975, including the offer to sell the regime nuclear-capable Jericho missiles. Israel also forgot that South Africa was supplying it with yellowcake uranium for its nuclear program. Worse still, is that when America and European countries had begun to abide by the UN arms embargo on the Apartheid regime, Israel happily continued in the trade.

For more facts, see *The Unspoken Alliance: Israel's Secret Relationship with Apartheid South Africa*, by senior editor of *Foreign Affairs* magazine Dr. Sasha Polakow-Suransky. The book uncovers many secret elements and details of the Israel–South Africa relationship. It traces the alliance between the two countries from the beginning of the Apartheid regime to its demise and the transition to majority rule. The worst part for Israel is its refusal to admit its shameful relationship with the defunct regime and its refusal to abide by international laws and treaties regarding the production, use, and proliferation of nuclear weapons.

Israel can only get away with its lies and deception by its reliance on the propaganda power of the wealthy American Zionist barons and the owners of the right wing media and press who made winning the argument against the war on Gaza impossible. They justified the unjustifiable blockade of Gaza, which is a collective punishment of 1.5 million civilians in the name of controlling the arms supply to Hamas. (That could have been the responsibility of the United Nations.) Under this pretence, they imposed a strictly limited supply of humanitarian goods and even the supply of toilet paper and fuel for heating and power generation, including materials such as cement and steel for the reconstruction of what the Israelis has destroyed during their indiscriminate bombardment. For more than three years of the blockade, the people of Gaza survived on goods smuggled from Egypt through hand-dug tunnels under the Israeli apartheid wall. Often, these tunnels were attacked by Israeli rockets killing and burying people within them.

The Israelis justify their evil actions by utilising their propaganda machine and every other available resource at their disposal, including their brilliance in turning adversity into advantage, in the same way they used the Holocaust to play and gain the Western world's sympathy that helped them occupy Palestine and displace its nation. The Holocaust also helped them obtain political and diplomatic advantage in America, where they ended up controlling its foreign policy. They were able to change the perception in America to the extent that the immoral and illegal actions of the extremist government in Israel are tolerated by the majority in American Congress. This is in contrast to the growing anti-Israel feeling in European countries, which is starting to evolve into anti-Semitism as a reaction to their arrogance and the inhumane treatment of the Palestinians.

The distinguished American historian Norman G. Finkelstein, in his books *The Holocaust Industry: Reflection on the Exploitation of Jewish Suffering* and *Beyond the Chutzpah: On the Misuse of Anti-Semitism and the Abuse of History* gives a good account of the lies that are aimed to mislead and distort the perception of the world's audience by ruthless propaganda. He argues that the Holocaust remembrance has been exploited by the Jewish establishment that constitutes a greater threat to the memory of the Holocaust than that of the Holocaust deniers, which he calls "the Holocaust industry." Finkelstein accuses those who exploit the Holocaust of telling lies and of naked greed. He argues that the ruthless industrialisation of the Holocaust has encouraged the rebirth of anti-Semitism in Europe and the United States. He makes it clear that the Holocaust industry is not about making sure that Nazi depravity is not forgotten, but is about extorting huge sums of money from Switzerland, Germany, and any other country which can be tarred with the Nazi brush. He indicts those who exploit the tragedy of the Holocaust for their own personal, political, and financial gain by documenting their cover-up of the blackmail of Swiss banks and the recent Holocaust compensation agreements. He concludes that the Holocaust industry has become an outright extortion racket.

He has never denied the Holocaust and that the Jews suffered terrible atrocities at the hand of the Nazis; he does, however, argue that Jews are not the only people in history to have suffered genocide and that the Jews' suffering shouldn't have given them the huge moral, political, and financial advantage they enjoy today, and most importantly, the advantage they are given to destroy the Palestinian nation by kicking them out of their homes. He cites human rights organisations such as Amnesty International, Human Rights Watch, and the Israeli human rights group B'Tselem and Breaking the Silence that document Israeli abuses in the occupied territories, including the killing of Palestinian civilians, torture of Palestinian prisoners, and home demolitions. More importantly, his arguments are accompanied with exhaustive research and detailed evidence on lethal disregard for Palestinian children and other non-combatants.

It is shame that human rights abuse and injustice in the occupied territories is so often ignored by the world and covered up by the right-wing media and press. How can the world ignore the lack of integrity of the Israeli Defence Force following the release of photographs showing Israeli soldiers posing alongside bound and gagged Palestinians prisoners? The release of photographs by the prominent Israeli advocacy group Breaking the Silence illustrates the widespread immoral and shameful culture that was tolerated by Israeli commanders who claim that the IDF has a moral and ethical code. The IDF ethical code must be similar to the American military code that allowed the disgraceful behaviour of American soldiers at Abu Ghraib and at Guantanamo Bay. According to Breaking the Silence, the organisation that documents the abuse of Palestinians by IDF soldiers countered the IDF claim about its ethical code saying, "The behaviour were the norm rather than an exception and the photographs were only the beginning as there were many thousands of similar photographs taken by Israeli soldiers." Furthermore, according to the Palestinian prisoner support and human right association, there were many more violations and abuses of Palestinians, without photographs. The Israeli newspaper *Ha'aretz* said the photos reflect a culture that has taken root in Israel that perceives Palestinian prisoners as sub-human. Unfortunately, these episodes show that the Israelis, corrupted by their power, can do anything they want to the Palestinians, which points to the deteriorated moral state of the Israeli army and its senior commanders, and not forgetting the moral state of the Israelis' unconditional backer, America.

The other aspect of Israeli inhumanity is the misery imposed on the Palestinian people and the collective punishment of Gaza's population.

Blockade of Gaza: The misery of the Palestinians has stirred the conscience of many European peace activists who have decided to help these powerless people by organising a flotilla of ships to deliver food and medicine through the Israeli blockade. It is easy to understand why the Free Gaza Movement wanted the blockade lifted and to raise international awareness about the virtual imprisonment of 1.5 million people in the Gaza Strip, where unemployment has soared to over 40 percent and power blackouts have become common. According to UN statistics, 70 percent of Gazans are living on less than a dollar a day, have no daily access to clean water, and rely on food aid. It is no wonder that the UN called the blockade "immoral and illegal." Even the loyal ally of Israel, the British Prime Minister David Cameron called the Palestinian territory of Gaza a "prison camp."

The Israeli brutality in Gaza was condemned by a group founded by Nelson Mandela that includes Nobel Peace Prize winner Desmond Tutu and former President Jimmy Carter in a statement that said, "The treatment of the people of Gaza is one of the world's greatest human rights violations and the blockade is not only illegal, it is counterproductive."

Despite all the misery, and while the world was watching, the Israelis on May 31, 2010 attacked the flotilla's flagship, the *Mavi Marmara* and killed nine men. This arrogant action provoked worldwide condemnation—except from America, which only expressed "deep regret."

Israeli action has breached international standards and human rights law through its use of armed force. The use of violence is prohibited unless it is strictly necessary, and the use of lethal force can only be justified in self-defence or to protect life. Questions have also been raised about Israel's violation of international maritime law, after reports that the flotilla was about 150 kilometers from Gaza's coast when attacked. The Free Gaza Movement has condemned the incident as an act of piracy. World reaction to Israel has provoked a rethink of the policy of shunning Hamas. Israel has faced a barrage of protests from around the world since its soldiers raided the flotilla of aid ships and began shooting at passengers. The Israeli government has arrogantly stood against the United Nations, NATO, and other world leaders who have condemned its actions.

Arab-Israeli parliamentarian Hanin Zoabi was on the flotilla when it was boarded by the Israeli commandos. Ms. Zoabi has diplomatic immunity from prosecution and was one of the first passengers freed. She said: "I watched what was happening from below deck and saw no provocation from those on board. The Israeli soldiers began to shoot while the helicopter was approaching." It is worth noting that Ms Zoabi was physically attacked by fellow members in the Knesset as she gave an account of the raid.

The attack on the flotilla prompted the United Nations Human Rights Council to adopt a resolution setting up an independent inquiry and condemning Israel's "outrageous attack."

In September 2010, a three-member UN human rights panel concluded that the Israeli commandos broke international law. The panel described the Israeli military response as "disproportionate" and a display of an unacceptable level of brutality. The panel's conclusion was that there is clear evidence to support prosecution for the willful killings and called the Israeli blockade of Gaza "unlawful."

In the 56-page report, the panel accuses Israeli forces of crimes, including violating the right to life, liberty, and freedom of expression, and of failing to treat prisoners with humanity. There was clear evidence to support prosecutions of the crimes within the terms of article 147 of the Fourth Geneva Convention.

To avoid total embarrassment, even the US has opened the door to international participation in the inquiry into Israel's interception of the flotilla, while at the same time vowing to continue its total support for Israel. (Cynically, and as expected, in January 2011, the Israeli-established inquiry cleared the Israeli government and the navy from any wrongdoing, while at the same time refusing to cooperate with the UN Human Right Council's inquiry.)

America's continued unconditional support for an extremist Israeli government is continuously undermining its contradictory and disingenuous efforts to reach out to the Muslim world. This is demonstrated by the Turkish government's dismay at the tepid nature of the US response to the tragedy, especially as Turkey is a staunch ally of America and the attacked ship in the flotilla was Turkish.

What has Israel achieved in intercepting the Free Gaza Movement flotilla? This act of stupidity is a kick in the teeth for Israel's diminishing friends, especially when Turkey was the only friend it had in the Islamic world. It claims it wants to be a normal member of the international community, but it behaves as a law unto itself, even in international waters.

It should be asked what danger the flotilla, with its humanitarian mission, posed to Israel?

Israel is a state that has the might of America behind it, receives extraordinary amounts of money and military hardware from America, and is now among the world's leading arms exporters and the only country in the Middle East to possess nuclear weapons. It is paradoxical behaviour from the so-called democratic Israel that denies freedom for the Palestinian people, steals their land, brings injustice to its citizens, and demolishes their homes to expand the Jewish settlements and condemn the Palestinian children to poverty.

Is there any decent leader left in Israel after the tragic assassination in 1995 of its Nobel Peace Price winner Prime Minister Yitzhak Rabin to lift the nation once more toward his noble aspirations, for which he sacrificed his life? Rabin was killed for being considered guilty by the extremist Zionists who became part of all Israeli governments since his assassination. The current Israeli leadership expects the world to believe that well trained, heavily armed Israeli commandos were so threatened by unarmed civilians that they needed to use deadly force. The Israeli government has more blood on its hands, and those who condone its criminal actions are as guilty as it is. It is ironic that when armed Somalis storm ships in international waters it is called piracy; the world's navies send ships to stamp it out. Will the world respond the same way when armed

Israelis storm ships in international waters and kill their occupants?

Unfortunately, the extremist Israeli government never hesitates to use its commandos and all its military might to achieve its sinister goals. In the process, it uses lies and deception to subvert world opinion. It often repeats the errors of history by constantly engaging in a savage repression of the Palestinian people and their right to a state of their own.

The blockade is a human catastrophe in the making for Gaza, a ghetto of despair for 1.5 million people. The International Red Cross reported that the Gazans continue to suffer the effects of siege-induced poverty and warfare. And as the Israeli novelist Amos Oz said, no idea has ever been defeated by force. Israelis should understand this better than any people on the planet but, tragically, their extremist religious nationalist leaders do not.

Perhaps an act of Israeli piracy on the high seas should've been a circuit-breaker for America to gain enough courage to stand up to Israel and change its foreign policy in the Middle East. However, the world is not holding its breath, because America's foreign policy is dictated by Israel.

On the other hand, the world condemnation of the attack on the flotilla, which has resulted in the partial lifting of the blockade on Gaza, can extend to the condemnation of Israel's inhumane treatment of the powerless Palestinians in their struggle to establish a just and viable state. It is only worldwide condemnation of Israel's brutality that has brought some temporary relief to Gaza's people. The temporary relief means that Gazans who live in an open-air prison may start rebuilding schools, hospitals, and homes destroyed by Israel.

However, the partial lifting of the blockade didn't impress the world humanitarian organisations, who are demanding the complete lifting of the blockade, the removal of the apartheid wall, and all Israeli-controlled crossings.

For more than three years, supermarkets in Gaza have relied on smuggled goods to stock their shelves. Under intense international pressure, Israel has agreed to ease the embargo on foods and goods allowed into Gaza, but human rights groups have branded Israel's move tokenism and window dressing and have demanded a complete end to the naval blockade, which is still in force. Hopefully, through the persistence of these humanitarian organisations, further overwhelming international pressure will result in the total lifting of the illegal and immoral blockade and the establishment of a viable state for the oppressed Palestinians.

It is worth noting that the blockade, which has deepened the poverty in Gaza, did not provoke an international outcry until Israeli commandos killed nine Turkish pro-Palestinian activists in international waters. In the process, Israel lost Turkey as its biggest Islamic friend. And as a result, Turkey became the new lifeline and inspiration for the so-called "Arab street," especially when Egypt and Saudi Arabia are considered by all Arabs as American and Israeli puppets.

The irony is that the Arabs will be more disappointed when they discover that Turkey is riddled with opportunism. Its obsession to join the European Union is driving it to show that it has major influence in the Middle East, which makes it beneficial to Europe. It should also be remembered that Turkey is another American puppet whose national interests coincide with the West, rather than with the Arabs. The Turkish government shows sympathy with the Palestinians through statements or sending some relief aid, but actually it recognises Israel, engages in trade, and carries out joint military training and shares information with it. Turkey, despite its pretence, was once and still is Israel's strongest ally with close military ties and a vigorous bilateral trade. In the wake of the 2008 Israeli assault on Gaza, however, ties between the two countries have temporarily cooled, but in late 2010, Turkey was actively seeking to restore the warm relations. Accordingly, Turkey cannot win the heart and mid of Arabs, unless it decides to place principles ahead of opportunism and stop prostituting itself between Europe and the Arab world.

Therefore, in the absence of a real champion to their cause, the Arab nations are now so desperate that they are left with no option but to resort to radicalism—a radicalism that America and Israel are sowing the seeds for and which will result in the eventual toppling of the puppet regimes in the Middle East. Sooner or later, the Arab revolt will be directed against their complacent leaders, especially against military dictatorships, which is now under way.

The assassination of Palestinian leaders: The frequent assassination of Palestinian leaders became worthy news only after the assassination by nearly thirty Israeli Mossad agents of Mahmoud al-Mabhouh in Dubai on 19 January 2010. What made the news worthy was not Israel's brutality, but the implication of Mossad agents illegally using fake and fraudulently obtained passports. Passports used by the assassins were from countries that are friends of Israel like Britain, Ireland, Australia, Germany, and France. Investigations by intelligence agencies had concluded that Israel was responsible for the abuse and counterfeiting of the fake passports.

Victor Ostrovsky, a former case officer at Mossad in the 1980s, stated that he has no doubt that passports have been forged or fraudulently used for similar operations in the past. They need foreign passports because they can't go around with an Israeli passport and get away or get involved with people from the Arab world. There were shelves upon shelves of real passports just waiting to be used. In his book, *By Way of Deception: The Making of Mossad officer* Ostrovsky writes of his experiences in the Mossad where he worked for many years. It was his love for Israel as a free and just country that made him ready to sacrifice his life, until he faced up to those who took it upon themselves to turn the Zionist dream into the present-day nightmare.

He describes Mossad's frightening and often ruthless covert activities around the world. In chilling detail, he asserts that the Mossad refused to share critical knowledge of a planned suicide mission in Beirut, leading to the death of hundreds of US Marines and French troops. He tells how they tracked Palestine Liberation Organisation

(PLO) chairman Yasser Arafat by recruiting his driver and bodyguard; how they withheld information on the whereabouts of American hostages, paving the way for the Iran-Contra scandal; and how their intervention into secret UN negotiations led to the sudden resignation of Ambassador Andrew Young and the downfall of his career. Ostrovsky describes the shocking scope and depth of the Mossad's influence, disclosing how Jewish communities in the US, Europe, and South America are armed and trained by the organisation in secret and how Mossad agents facilitate the drug trade in order to pay the enormous costs of its far-flung clandestine operations.

Assassination, kidnapping, deportation, and imprisonment of Palestinian leaders were going on for many years when Israel, through its propaganda machine, was justifying its behaviour by branding the Palestinians as terrorists. Unfortunately, the West came to accept that Israeli state terrorism was "okay" and reaction to it "not okay." It seems that people whose land is occupied by a foreign force have no right to resist, but must surrender gracefully.

The West seems to forget that the French, the Greek, the Yugoslav, and the Italian resistance fighters during World War II were considered heroes. The West seems to forget that the Palestinian resistance consists of stone-throwing and the odd primitive rockets. Worse still, this resistance is enclosed within a concrete wall whilst the occupying invader is equipped with the latest technologies, including tanks, helicopters, satellites, drones, electronically guided missiles, etc. This was evident from the last war on Gaza when Israel was bombing, burning, and killing many innocent people without any resistance or counterattack by the Palestinians.

The killing of Palestinian leaders should shift the focus to state terrorism, which places Israel in a position parallel to the very forces it has often unfailingly condemned as terrorist groups or networks. This is not the first time, and may not be the last, that a state has engaged in such an operation. In the case of Israel, specifically, it has historically never shied away from targeting those it has regarded as a threat to its national interests. In this, it has never made an allowance for those who have sought to defend themselves against Israel's brutality or to free themselves from its territorial-strategic expansion and physical subjugation.

This form of terrorism has a long history in the Middle East and Israel was and is at the centre of it. It began with the founders of Israel, led by David Ben-Gurion, who showed no moral qualms about forming the first nationalistic terrorist groups such as the Stern Gang and Irgun (Irgun was led by Menachem Begin, a terrorist who later became a prime minister) in the 1930s to terrorise the British out of Palestine and create the state of Israel in 1948 on what had traditionally been recognised as Palestinian land. Israel has justified all this and related activities, including sealing off and punishing Palestinians in Gaza, the West Bank, and East Jerusalem. It did that in the name of its right to exist, but against all international legal and humanitarian norms and standards. It has totally disregarded the right of the Palestinian people to self-determination and rejected any ruling of the International Court of Justice. It has arrogantly stood up to pressure from the Obama administration to halt the expansion of Israeli settlements in the West Bank and East Jerusalem.

It is time for the international community, specifically those states friendly to Israel, including America and Britain, to condemn it, as they should condemn any state terrorism, and put pressure on it to behave within international norms and laws. Israel might thus stop being a delinquent actor with only a claim of being democratic in world politics. America itself, in the name of fighting terrorism, is killing many innocent people without being accountable. America's past wars, including Vietnam and the Iraq wars, had the elements of state terrorism.

Resistance to state terrorism is fully justified as it is part of natural human behaviour. Aggression provokes resistance and violence breeds violence.

Extremism of Yisrael Beiteinu Party (Israel Our Home Party):

The ruthlessness of Israel can be demonstrated by the election of the Likud Party and its coalition partner the Yisrael Beiteinu Party, a racist party led by Avigdor Lieberman, which was established in 1999. Lieberman is the Israeli foreign minister and deputy prime minister in Netanyahu's religious nationalist far-right government, which was formed in March 2009. Despite his open racism, his inclusion in the cabinet has failed to elicit any significant protest nationally or internationally. Instead, he has been welcomed by influential Jewish institutions such as the Brookings Saban Centre, where he participated in a forum alongside Bill and Hillary Clinton.

To illustrate his extremism it is worth noting the following:

- In 2001, he proposed that the West Bank be divided into four cantons, with no central Palestinian government and no possibility for Palestinians to travel between the cantons.
- In 2002, he said that the Palestinians should be given an ultimatum that "at 8 a.m. we'll bomb all their commercial centres and at noon we'll bomb their gas stations and at 2 p.m. we'll bomb their banks."
- In 2003, he said that the thousands of Palestinian prisoners held by Israel should be drowned in the Dead Sea and he offered to provide the buses to take them there.
- In 2004, he called for the transfer of Israeli territory with Palestinian populations to the Palestinian Authority. Likewise, Israel would annex the major Jewish settlement blocs on the Palestinian West Bank. If applied, his plan would strip roughly one-third of Israel's Palestinian citizens of their citizenship. A loyalty test would be applied to those who desired to remain in Israel. This plan to trade territory with the Palestinian Authority is a revision of his earlier calls for the forcible transfer of Palestinian citizens of Israel from their land.

- Also in 2004, he said that 90 percent of Israel's 1.2 million Palestinian citizens would have to find a new Arab country in which to live beyond Israel's borders as they have no place here. "They can take their bundles and get lost."
- In 2006, he called for the killing of Arab members of Knesset who meet with members of the Hamas-led Palestinian Authority.

It is interesting to note that earlier, in 1998, he called for the flooding of Egypt by bombing the Aswan Dam in retaliation for Egyptian support for Yasser Arafat.

This is the man who represents the face of Israel on the international stage when the Western World's conscience has gone to sleep.

It is a double standard in _No_ reaction to Avigdor Lieberman's above statements compared to the savage reaction to statements made by Helen Thomas in June 2010, in which she said, "Israel should get the hell out of Palestine" and her further suggestion that the Israelis go home to Germany, Poland, or the United States.

By not reacting to the extremist Lieberman's statements, it gives the indication that: First, the majority of the journalistic fraternity is hostage to their right-wing masters, who control the media and the press with their power of hiring and firing, which leaves most journalists little room to speak their mind. How for example can journalists (with some exceptions) who are embedded with the troops be totally objective if they stand no chance of an impact reporting on troops' atrocities, especially when their own safety and survival depend on them turning blind eye or even covering up?

This aspect of journalism was clearly demonstrated by a video showing the killing in Iraq by an American military strike of two Reuter's journalists and many civilians that was kept a secret for two years by the embedded *Washington Post* journalist David Finkel, who came across the dead and wounded soon after the helicopters fired. Finkel has never publicly disclosed whether he had the video or not. The video came to light only after it was leaked by government whistle-blowers to WikiLeaks, which was released under the name of "Collateral Murder." The whistle-blowers within the government felt, according to WikiLeaks, that the atmosphere around the killings was overly relaxed.

<u>Second</u>, public opinion in turn is a hostage to the propaganda that is dished out by powerful vested interests. The lack of independent media and press makes a mockery of the so-called American democratic system. Independent and fearless writers, movie makers and journalists of the calibre of Julian Assange, Daniel Ellsberg, Michael Moore, Robert Fisk, and John Pilger are a diminishing breed. This has resulted in democracy becoming hostage to the power of money, which is in the hands of the right and the extreme-right groups.

In their book *Manufacturing Consent: The Political Economy of the Mass Media,* Noam Chomsky and Edward S. Herman analyse the media as a business for profit. As such their distortion of news, what type of news, which items, and how they are reported is motivated by profit rather than public interest. When accuracy over profit fails, the items are relegated to a lower margin proportional to their market value.

The media, for example, is not interested in promoting non-violent conflict resolution because reporting violent conflicts is more profitable. It appears that the more violent the conflict is, the bigger the media profit, which makes it hostage to vested interests and its bottom line. Because of this, peace reporting is also relegated to a lower margin. In the process of reporting violent conflicts, the media determine who the goodies are and who the baddies are, and who deserves to live and who deserve to die. In the process, many journalists follow their media masters in playing down, ignoring, or justifying the catastrophic humanitarian, economic, political, and environmental consequences of conflicts.

In *Media Control: The Spectacular Achievement of Propaganda* Chomsky writes, "Honesty leaves us with a dilemma. The easy answer is conventional hypocrisy. The other option is the one adopted by our media."

This is where the importance of honest journalists, filmmakers, commentators and writers should be highlighted as a beacon of light to others:

Julian Assange: The founder of the website WikiLeaks is an unpaid volunteer, a prominent media spokesman, and the website director. In 2009, he was the winner of the Amnesty International Media Award (New Media). In February 2011, he was awarded Sydney Peace Medal by the

Sydney Peace Foundation, Australia. In the same month, he was nominated for the 2011 Noble Peace Prize for his promotion of human rights. His aim is to create a system where there is guaranteed free press across the world, ensuring that every individual in the world has the ability to publish materials that are meaningful. He sees his role primarily related to the safety of individual human beings rather than the safety of the state. He describes himself as a combative person who likes stopping people who have created victims from creating any more. He expresses disdain for the military by alluding to a statement attributed to Albert Einstein, a noted pacifist, who describes soldiers as contemptible drones and attacks patriotism as a cover for brutality and war.

Despite the orchestrated campaign against him, more secret revelations by his website are assured. The secretive and vested interests forces are out to silence one of the essential sources of information for people who are lied to by their manipulative governments. As a matter of fact, if these governments were honest with their people, WikiLeaks wouldn't need to exist.

No matter what, Julian Assange, please never give up, you must know that all free-thinking people are behind you and behind your stand to promote justice.

Daniel Ellsberg: A former United States military analyst who released the Pentagon Papers on American government decision making during the Vietnam War. The US government, despite knowing all along that the war would not likely be won, continued to sacrifice casualties without admitting the fact publicly. Additionally, high-ranking officials had disregard for the loss of life and injury suffered by soldiers and civilians. The irony is that the Americans and their allies know that the war in Afghanistan equally cannot be won, yet they continue fighting with disregard to the loss of more of their soldiers and the killing of more civilians.

Ellsberg continued his political activism against the invasion of Iraq, countering the Bush administration's pro-war propaganda campaign.

John Pilger: An Australian journalist and documentary filmmaker. He has received human rights and journalism awards, the Sydney Peace Prize, and was twice a winner of Britain's Journalist of the Year Award. He was described by Noam Chomsky as a beacon of light in often dark times. He was a war correspondent in Vietnam, Cambodia, Egypt, India, Bangladesh, and Biafra who later became a documentarian. His first of many documentaries was *The Quiet Mutiny*, in which he revealed the shifting morale and the open rebellion of Western troops against the Vietnam War. He is a staunch critic of many aspects of America's foreign policy, which he regards as being driven by a largely imperialist agenda. His courage and insight is a constant inspiration to others. He is the voice for those without a voice and a journalist universally recognised.

Michael Moore: A liberal political commentator, filmmaker, and author. He is well known for his film *Fahrenheit 9/11*, one of the highest rated documentaries of all time. His writing and filmmaking stand out in his criticism of large corporations, ownership of offensive weapons, globalisation, and the war in Iraq. In *Fahrenheit 9/11*, he examines America after the attack on the World Trade Center and establishes the alleged link of the Bush family with Osama bin Laden. The film was awarded the Palme d'Or, the top honour at the 2004 Cannes Film Festival.

Helen Thomas: An American journalist and author who was a member of the White House Press Corps, she served fifty-seven years until her resignation on June 7, 2010, as a consequence of her comment about Israel and the Palestinians. She was the first woman in the National Press Club, first female member and president of the White House Correspondents' Association, and covered the period from Eisenhower to the second year of the Obama administration. One of her popular quotes concerns George W. Bush. When once asked why she was sad, she said, "I'm covering the worst president in American history."

Her downfall however, is an illustration of the Jewish lobby groups' clout in America. She dared to criticise the untouchables who defend the indefensible atrocities of Israel against the Palestinians.

During her career she received many awards, including the Helen Thomas Lifetime Achievement Award from The White House Correspondents' Association, Foremother Award from the National Research Center for Women & Families, the Helen Thomas Spirit of Diversity award from Wayne State University, and the William Allen White Foundation Award for Journalistic Merit from the University of Kansas.

Robert Fisk: An English writer and journalist and a Middle East correspondent of the *Independent*. He holds many British and international journalism awards. One of his famous sayings is, "Journalism must challenge authority, all authority, especially so when governments and politicians take us to war." He once said, "There is a misconception that journalists can be objective ... What journalism is really about is to monitor power and the centre of power." He received a BA in English Literature at Lancaster University in 1968 and a PhD in Political Science, from Trinity College, Dublin, in 1983.

All the above and many other highly principled journalists, writers, philosophers, filmmakers, and political activists deserve our admiration: "We salute you!"

Chapter 6

Religion: The Cause of America's Demise

The war on Islam and the entrenchment of Christian fundamentalism will lead to America's demise

The Evangelical and the Religious Right Groups

The far-right religious groups such as the Assemblies of God and the Christian Right televangelists are mostly dominionists who subscribe to an apocalyptic "End of Times" theology. The term "dominionism" is used to describe the growing political influence of the Christian Rights and as a social/political movement. It is a movement of fundamentalists who are politically active, seeking to dominate the political process as part of a mandate from God. Their doctrine is based on the Bible's text in Genesis 1:26: "And God said; let us make man in our image, after our likeness: and let them have dominion over the fish of the sea, and over the fowl of the air, and over the cattle, and over all the earth, and over every creeping thing that creeps upon the earth."

The fundamentalist dominionists believe that Christians alone are biblically mandated to occupy all secular institutions until Christ returns. Christian Right televangelists such as Pat Robertson make frequent use of "dominion language" by adopting the idea of taking dominion over the secular institutions of the United States as the "central unifying ideology" of their social movement. They decided to gain political power through the Republican Party by bringing Christians and Jews into the government on the basis that there will never be world peace until God's house and God's people are given their rightful place of leadership.

Dominion theology extremism is reflected in the claim that Christian men with specific theological beliefs are ordained by God to run society. Christians and others who do not accept their theological beliefs would be second-class citizens.

It is unfortunate for America and the rest of the world that these radical religious-right groups have succeeded in converting the Republican Party into a party of theocracy through which they are driving American politics, using God on almost every issue: crime and punishment, foreign policy, health care, taxation, energy, regulation, social services, and so on. Their greatest enemy is a secular government and anybody who advocates for a secular government. This theocracy is indistinguishable from an extreme Islamic fundamentalism in which religion and politics are inseparable.

Their success will certainly cause America's demise.

The evangelical movement's support of Zionism stems from their belief that people of the Jewish religion will return to Israel in order to hasten the second coming of Christ, which will convert the Jews to Christianity. This is why the term "Christian Zionism" is now often used to describe Christians supporting Israel. The beliefs of these fanatics are sourced from their interpretation of the Book of Revelation, the last book of the New Testament, which is also called Apocalypse of John.

The people of the Jewish religion in the meantime are playing a game of using these fanatic Christians to their advantage by displacing millions of innocent people, demolishing their houses and grabbing their land, whilst they live happily with the knowledge that Christ has gone and will never come back.

It is easy to understand why the smart Jews don't believe in the fantasy of the second coming of Christ, as it is based on a fairy tale of Jesus will come from heaven to earth when all the dead will be resurrected and the last judgment of all the living and the dead will take place and then the Kingdom of God will be established and God will Reign. **Don't be so sure!**

The joke however, will be on the extremist Jews when the evangelicals and other religious-right groups discover that they have been used by the religious nationalist Jews for political, moral, and material gain. All hell then will break loose and a new savage round of anti-Semitism will be driven by the dominionists and the Tea Party movement.

The signs of incipient anti-Semitism are becoming clearer, for example in Sarah Palin's statement in January 2011 following the shooting of Congresswoman Gabrielle Giffords. In answering her critics she used the expression "blood libel" to imply that the media were out to get her. The expression "blood libel" has been used for centuries against Jews, often to malign them as child murderers who coveted the blood of Christian children. Blood libel has been a central fable of anti-Semitism in which Jews have been accused of using the blood of Gentile children for medicinal purposes or to mix in with matzo, or unleavened bread, traditionally eaten at Passover.

The spread of the accusation of blood libel dates to the Middle Ages and has been a factor in the murder or even massacre of Jews. The term carries particular power among Jews, though it has taken on other meanings. One of the first recorded tragedies attributed to blood libel occurred in the twelfth century, when a boy named William in Norwich, England, was found dead with stab wounds. Jews were accused of killing him in ritual fashion and several sources say most of the Jewish population was then wiped out in a massacre. Allegations of blood libel spread during the Nazi Germany.

Unfortunately, the evangelicals and other religious-right groups are now identified strongly with the grassroots of the Tea Party movement, which is triggering the resurgence of the Republican Party and bringing fear to the hearts of civil libertarians with their extreme conservative views. Returning the Republican Party to the era of the born-again George W. Bush and taking it further to the right will provoke an uglier reaction against America, especially from the Islamic world.

It was not long ago when George W. Bush, apparently a Christian Zionist, brought Paul Wolfowitz and Douglas Feith and other Jewish extremist religious nationalists into his administration with total knowledge of their agenda. Before hiring, it is usual for federal agencies to perform exhaustive security clearance checks on all recruits to sensitive national security areas of the government, which means the administration had to know exactly what their agenda was before hiring them. Christian Zionists' belief in supporting Israel's expansionist policies on biblical grounds is exactly what American Jewish Zionists needed to advance Israel's cause. As a result, the world has witnessed the invasion of Iraq and as a result of that, the Americans are suffering from increased terrorism. Furthermore, as demanded by Israel, the invasion of Iran and Syria is now in the planning stage. (See Chapter 5.) The suffering will gradually lead the Americans to discover the reason behind their country's decline and what constitutes the biggest threat to America.

Most religious leaders' survival largely depends on entangling religion with politics to allow them to use religion for lobbying purposes. They engage in political activity in a variety of ways, including national media campaigns and grassroots organisations aimed at supporting particular candidates in elections and using mail and phone calls to reach office-holders. They are now heavily involved in presidential elections and national politics, while continuing to pursue specific issues at lower levels of government. Nationally, they encourage electoral participation among their members and use registration drives to enroll church-goers to vote for their endorsed candidates.

They achieve their religious objectives by combining their fundamentalism with their charisma to manipulate the ignorant section of society, especially in their ability to apply mass psychology on the unaware through mega-churches. Their action became lethal when they joined forces with the extreme Zionists to elect George W. Bush as president, which became an awful part of America's history. It was a history of conflict and destruction that the world will rue for many years to come.

It is worth noting that many of the evangelical churches were pacifist until 1967 when they decided to adopt their new position of affirming their loyalty to the government of the United States in war or peace. Prior to 1967, the Assemblies of God, along with the majority of other Pentecostal denominations, officially opposed Christian participation in war and considered themselves a "for peace and non-violence" organisations. Unfortunately however, their participation in many elections, including the election of George W. Bush and their commitment to the warmongering Republican Party has proven them to support violence. Currently they are leading the way, together with the extremist Zionists, in their venomous campaign against Islam.

Their interpretation of prophecies in the Apocalypse of John and the second coming of Christ and catastrophic end-time event have destructive consequences. The clash of Christianity and the secular governments as part of God's intervention to save mankind from self-destruction and the establishment of God's government by ending man's self-rule can lead the world into a catastrophe. The ridiculous aspect of the prophecy is the killing of billions of people to save them from self-destruction that doesn't add up, especially when considering that humans have proven over millennia to be rational thinkers equipped with the natural instincts of survival and self-preservation.

Their religious delusions should not be allowed to drive American politics, especially when America is meant to be a secular country where constitutionally, religion and state are separated. To be guided by religious dogma that is based on conjectures is dangerous to America and to humanity.

It is amazing to see some evangelicals at gatherings of the Tea Party call for the support of the military and a return to God by asking their followers to get on their knees and pray for redemption and to rebuild America's sacred honour. These people don't understand that they themselves destroyed America's honour and its economy by pushing it into wars that stand no chance of being won and that result in the killing of many innocent people, including women and children. America's honour can be restored by respecting other countries' sovereignty and by dealing with the world on a win-win basis, rather than a winner-takes-all basis. America's honour can also be restored by reigning in Israeli aggression and its expansionism at the expense of the Palestinians.

Zionism

Zionism is a religious nationalistic movement for the return of the Jewish people to their homeland and the resumption of Jewish sovereignty in the land of Israel. It was founded by Theodor Herzl (1860–1904), a Hungarian visionary sometimes called the father of modern Zionism and the state of Israel. Only after his death was a decision reached to colonise Palestine as an Israeli state on the grounds of its biblical connection. As the land was occupied by "strangers" the organisers believed that anyone not Jewish had no right to be there. The Zionists created the myth that **Palestine is a land without people for a people without a land**. Based on these ideological roots, the Zionists sought the complete dispossession of the Arab's land to re-establish the biblical land of Israel.

An estimated 30,000 Jewish immigrants from Eastern Europe and Yemen arrived in Palestine between 1881 and 1903. This group constituted the first wave of migrants who laid the foundation for further settlements in Palestine. The second wave of 40,000 Jewish migrants from Russia and Poland arrived between 1904 and 1914. World War I began in 1914, when Palestine was under the control of the Ottoman Empire. On July 24, 1922, Palestine came under British control following official confirmation by the Council of the League of Nations, which took effect on September 26, 1923. Under the mandate of administration of Palestine, the British, based on their Balfour promise of 1917, proceeded to establish a Jewish homeland, which heralded the beginning of relentless displacement and suffering of the indigenous Palestinians. This is despite the clear British original intention in establishing a Jewish homeland was to ensure not to prejudice the rights of the Palestinians.

It is worth noting that the terms *Zionistic, Zionist* and *Zionism* were coined in1890 by Dr. Nathan Birnbaum (1864–1937). He later tagged the term *political Zionism* (1892). Birnbaum was born in Vienna and lived there till1908. In 1882, together with two other students at the University of Vienna, he founded Kadima, the first organisation of Jewish nationalist students in the West. In 1897 he was elected secretary-general of the Zionist organisation. He was one of the most important representatives of the cultural rather than the political side of Zionism. However, he left the organisation not long after the First Zionist Congress (held in1897). He broke with the political Zionism of Herzl because he thought the Jewish nation was not merely a group of people held together by a common enemy and that its survival could not be secured by political concessions in Palestine. His thoughts were in contradiction with Herzl's ideology of colonising Palestine. He was unhappy with the negative view of Diaspora Jewry and the transformation of the Zionist ideals into a party machine. His main focus was to advocate Jewish cultural autonomy, focusing in particular on the Jews of Eastern Europe. He advocated that the Jews be recognised as a people among the other peoples of the Austrian Empire, with Yiddish as their official language.

In his books *The Ethnic Cleansing of Palestine* and *A History of Modern Palestine: One Land, Two People*, the Israeli historian Ilan Pappe traces the roots of Zionism from the time of its inception in Europe to modern times, including the establishment of the Jewish state and its ethnic cleansing of Palestinians. From the beginning, the Palestinians knew that a Jewish state meant Jewish migration and that therefore their land needed to be protected through strong opposition to Jewish settlements. The Palestinians' opposition came to nothing because it didn't coincide with the British plans for Palestine that culminated in the establishment of the Jewish state in 1948, when the Palestinians lost their homeland. This is the year when the Palestinians constituted over 80 percent of the population and when the minority Zionist settlers received preferential treatment. Earlier, since their mandate, the British had been helping the settlers to transform the settlers' paramilitary organisation into a military arm of the Zionist governing body, which later became the Israel Defence Forces (IDF).

Under the leadership of the first Israeli Prime Minister, David Ben-Gurion, the Zionist movement set out to cement Jewish sovereignty over most of Palestine in any way possible, including the forceful removal of millions of Palestinians from their land and to replace them with Jewish settlers. To achieve their goals, the Zionists used a systematic plan to cleanse the land by compulsory transfer of land to Jewish settlers. The forceful removal of millions of Palestinians from their land contradicted the original Zionist's myth that "**Palestine is a land without people for a people without a land.**"

For the Palestinians, the loss of their land to the Zionists in 1948 was a catastrophe equal to the Jewish Holocaust. The catastrophe was deepened during Arab-Israeli war when over 700,000 Palestinians fled or were deported from their homes. The Palestinians use the term "Nakba," meaning "disaster," to describe this catastrophe.

Pappe argues that it was deliberately planned ethnic cleansing and a crime against humanity, rather than a circumstance of war, which occurred and continues to the present day and that it was part of a long-standing Zionist plan to manufacture an ethnically pure Jewish state. His argument in using the term "ethnic cleansing" is based on United Nations definitions. He gives detailed accounts of Israeli military involvement in the demolition and depopulation of many villages and the expulsion of many thousands of Palestinians, which continues today. Pappe calls for the unconditional return of all Palestinian refugees and the end of the Israeli occupation.

It is worth noting that in 1975 the UN General Assembly adopted a resolution slandering Zionism by equating it with racism. However, under pressure from America, the resolution was repealed in 1991.

Zionism is a movement developed by a group of religious nationalists who used their manipulative power to further their dubious agenda. It is an ideology based on the claim that God gave land in the Middle East to the Jewish people four thousand years ago. The claim is not sustainable for the fact that the majority of Jewish people today have no relationship to the Jews of four thousand years ago, other than in their religious belief. This fact alone makes a mockery of the idea that a portion of land in the Middle East belongs by divine fiat to the Jews of today.

Zionism is a cancer capable of spreading and infecting many parts of the body by attaching itself to many organs that are capable of destruction. Currently, the Zionist ideology is in the process of destroying America. The destruction of America in turn will lead to the destruction of Zionism.

In his book *Zionism Is the Real Enemy of the Jews*, the former Middle East chief correspondent for Independent Television News Alan Hart has succeeded in telling the world of the immediate and long-term dangers involved in unconditional Western support for Zionism and its oppressive policies against the Palestinians. He exposes the fact that unconditional Western support for Israel will endanger the existence of the Jewish state by fuelling anti-Semitism, not only in Islamic countries but around the world. The tragedy in the Middle East perpetrated by extremist Zionists is not only for Palestinians, but for the Israelis themselves and the rest of the world. Analytically, through his in-depth research, Hart explains the threat of Zionism. His research also confirms what was stated earlier that Zionism is owned and promoted by manipulative and extremist religious group that is linked to AIPAC.

In another book by professor Rosemary Radford and political scientist Herman Ruether entitled *The Wrath of Jonah: The Crisis of Religious Nationalism in the Israeli-Palestinian Conflict*, the writers argue that Israel and America, not the Palestinians, are the chief obstacles to peace in the Middle East. The authors believe that the Palestinians' implicit recognition of Israel's right to exist has to be accepted in good faith without the need for waiting and using the waiting time as an excuse to grab more of the Palestinians' land. For a just solution to the conflict, the authors admirably propose the rejection of fanaticism in Judaism, Islam, and Christianity and the formation of an ethnic solidarity between Jews, Muslims, and Christians. To achieve peace in the Middle East, the Palestinians must be treated justly.

The Israeli-Palestinian conflict is "a story of two tragedies"—the Palestinian uprooting and suffering as refugees, and the moral debacle of the Jewish state itself.

The religious nationalism of Muslims and Jews, the Christian Zionists' support for Israel, and the creation of the Jewish state are the main causes of the conflict in the Middle East and the main reason for the rise of terrorism and anti-Semitism around the world. As a solution to the conflict, it is necessary for the Israeli occupier and oppressor of the Palestinians to make some political and territorial compromises towards achieving a satisfactory two-state solution.

The forced segregation of a nation, and surrounding them with a concrete wall, is a sign of a corrupted human spirit and a violation of the lowest code of ethics. If Zionism stands for colonisation, oppression, and apartheid, it must be condemned by all fair-minded people. It must be condemned when listening to Rabbi Ovadia Yosef, the spiritual leader of one of Israel's ruling parties, who appealed to God to inflict the plague on the Palestinian president before the start of new peace talks in Washington in August 2010. He also said, "May all the nasty people who hate Israel vanish from our world" and added,

"May God strike them down with the plague, along with all Palestinians who persecute Israel." Extremist Zionists never refrain from inciting hatred and violence against the Palestinians. Again, it is through the interpretation of religion, and the approbation of so-called religious righteousness, that causes the fragmentation and conflicts in the world.

Zionism, which inspired the stateless and persecuted Jewish people to search for a homeland, has ended up trampling the rights of Palestinians.

Professor Jacqueline Rose, in her book *The Question of Zion* analyses the identity of Zionism and its rigidity as an ideology. Rose also highlights the role of the dissidents of Zionism who strongly believe in the legitimate claims of the Palestinians, which Israel must meet before it can transform itself. Rose criticises Israel for linking the Holocaust and the founding of the Jewish state in a way that justifies Israel's policies, which are driven by the extremist settlers in their quest to grab Palestinian land. Her book questions the merit of religious nationalism and the concept of religious redemption and national liberation which is at the heart of the Arab-Israeli conflict. It is the Jewish settlers' fanatical adherence to the concept of the "Promised Land" and by not giving any concession to the Palestinians means the end of the process of Jewish redemption. It is destroying their spiritual foundation, as there is no middle ground or offer of equality for the oppressed Palestinians. And in the name of anti-terrorism they have succeeded in implementing their brutal agenda in the occupied territories.

Israel tries to present the Jews as a disadvantaged people, despite its extremely violent stance towards the Palestinians in the process of implementing the Zionist project. It acts with impunity on the ground of self-defence, when in fact it is the provocateur, the aggressor, and the occupier of Palestinian land. The self-defence argument is the most powerful propaganda tool currently in use, one that makes it and America more comfortable to hide behind. **Please wake up!**

Islamic Revolt

The war on Islam is creating a class of people that have nothing left to lose. Perhaps America and Israel assume that these people eventually will have no option but to surrender. Instead, the world is now witnessing the fact that these people are standing up to fight.

The current relentless wave of discrimination against Muslims in the Western world is fuelled by politicians and vested interests, which will ultimately destroy the social fabric of their countries and will have a devastating effect on international relations. Creating 1.5 billion despised people targeted as the enemy will never lead to world peace, but to a protracted war for many generations to come.

The Islamophobia that was started by George W. Bush following the September 11 attacks in his statement about a "war of civilisation" has spread into many Western countries where discrimination against Muslims is now the norm rather than the exception. A constant barrage of bullies, media messages, and some personalities (See Chapter 2) of authority who demean Muslims because of their faith are having a devastating effect on the morale of this social group, the majority of whom are law-abiding and moderate citizens.

Islamophobia is hostility and discrimination against Muslims in their exclusion from mainstream political and social life. Anti-Semitism is now extended against all Arabs who became the subject of racial profiling and intolerance.

The disgraceful behaviour of some extremist religious and political leaders in their attempt to marginalise some sectors of their community will eventually cause resentment and revolt. Pushing these people into the corner and subjecting them to humiliation through no fault of their own is motivating them to fight for their dignity and survival. History is littered with examples of nations that have not benefited from fragmentation. As discussed in Chapter 2, subjecting Muslims in America to the same treatment that was once applied to African Americans can only create second-class citizens with nothing left to lose but to turn violent or be recruited by violent organisations. Promoting irrational fear and hatred against a group of people because of an aspect of their identity or their belief is a recipe for bullying and institutionalised discrimination. Politicians and religious leaders who engage in spreading fear and hatred for temporary gains of popularity are guilty of bringing long-term harm to the social harmony that should be enjoyed by future generations.

Some leaders insist on highlighting only the dark side of interpretation of Islam, adding their own interpretation, and taking things out of context and purposely ignoring the dark side of their own interpretation of Christianity and Judaism. The Constitution, meant to promote equality and ethical human relations, fails miserably in the face of bigotry, prejudice, and blatant discrimination. Isn't the soul of Western countries founded on the unity of people from different ethnic and religious backgrounds living together? It appears that the world needs a new leader like Martin Luther King Jnr. to remind it of social justice and human rights principles, the anchor of a civilised society.

The West has a choice to treat other religious and ethnic groups as equals and to make them fight for peace or to treat them as despised and make them fight for their dignity and survival. There is nothing in the world that can categorise people as pure after been indoctrinated, except for when they are born. They are all born equal, until they are brainwashed to become good citizens or criminals or bigots or terrorists. Fanaticism and terrorism associated with prejudice, racism, and bigotry are common in all nations and are usually fuelled by extremist leaders who are well-trained in mind control. The success of these abhorrent leaders is directly related to the level of social ignorance and to the power of their manipulation.

It is worth noting that the Old Testament endorses the killing of anybody who incites you to worship another god because of our jealous God. However, treating others the way you want to be treated appears more realistic and easier to fulfill.

Convincing white Christian Americans that Muslims and black Americans are equally entitled to citizenship as they are and regardless of their faith or the colour of their skin should be an easy task if not for some extremist religious and political leaders whose survival largely depends on fragmenting society and creating conflict. Unfortunately, knowingly or unknowingly, these leaders are driving America to its demise by promoting discrimination on the grounds of race, religion, nationality, or ethnic origin that entail having limited access to employment, education, housing, and goods and services. Marginalisation of minority groups usually causes resentment and brings out the worse in people.

It stands to reason that if all religious and political leaders are enlightened and united on the subject of equality, society will be harmonious. This criterion applies to all countries with population from various racial, religious, ethnic, and social backgrounds.

Intolerance of and discrimination against Muslims has become increasingly prevalent in America and other Western countries, which manifests itself in harassment, hate speeches, and violent attacks and distorted representations of Islam and Muslim communities in the media and in many political forums.

Through no fault of Arab Americans and Muslim citizens, following the September 11 attacks, they became victims of demonisation, hatred, racism, and discrimination.

Religious Nationalism

If religion is the opiate of the people, religious nationalism is their death-bed.

Throughout human history, millions of people have died in the name of religion and nationalism; when combined, they are dynamite. In promoting religious nationalism, political and religious leaders employ mass psychology to convince people that their primary duty and loyalty is to the superiority of their nation-state and God. They glorify many aspects of religious and national virtues that develop into a euphoric love of the nation and the exclusion of the rights of other nations, which results in conflicts, as has been exemplified in the rise of fascism in Nazi Germany that led to World War II.

Religious nationalistic leaders usually produce extremist sentiment by coupling their religious traditions to their land and ethnicity. These leaders promote the political idea that the faith of the group is privileged at the expense of others, or they promote the idea of revolt against or rejection of others under well-crafted nationalistic banners. Throughout history, religious nationalism has often led to the domination of one group over another, often achieved through violence and violation of human rights.

The Crusades, the troubles in Ireland, the Israeli-Palestinian conflict, the ethnic-religious conflict in Iraq, and conflicts or wars in Chechnya, Nigeria, Burundi, Ivory Coast, Iran, Afghanistan, Kashmir, and Sri Lanka offer some examples of the negative effect of religious nationalism.

At the root of the current Arab-Israeli conflict is religious nationalism. The intermittent armed conflict and the constant psychological warfare are mainly aimed at the destruction of each others' religious nationalistic feeling that constitutes the major stumbling block for peaceful resolution. The dynamics of the conflict are embodied in the winner-takes-all principle, which provokes resistance, a fight for survival, and endless war. Israel currently has the upper hand because of America's unconditional support, but with the decline of America or in the event that America comes to the conclusion that Israel is a total liability to its national interest, the balance of power may shift to favour the Arabs.

Israel's expansionist policies at the expense of the Palestinians are focusing the world's attention on its sponsor, America. As a result, America is creating more enemies not only throughout the Arab countries, but throughout the world. Additionally, many European countries that suffered the consequences of German nationalism during World War II are gradually becoming more sympathetic to the plight of the Palestinians. It is becoming obvious that Israel is gradually but inevitably heading for an ultra-religious nationalism which is likely to culminate in further ethnic cleansing and genocide against the Palestinians. The relentless ethnic cleansing in Jerusalem and the genocide of innocent Palestinians in Gaza occur while the world turns a blind eye—just as it did before the rise of Nazi Germany. The world is well aware of German fascism as a national collectivism that unified Germany under the banner of growth and expansion. The Jews also are well aware of the Holocaust.

Moderate Jews should be alarmed by the behaviour of their extremist leaders and must ensure that these leaders are prevented from doing to the Palestinians what Nazi Germany did to the Jews. And something else: The Jews should never get encouraged by the current Christian nationalistic war against Islam, because first, such a war cannot be won and second, Christian nationalism could potentially turn out to be a lethal weapon against Zionism.

Christian nationalists gain their popularity by identifying their enemies, currently the Muslim radicals they have targeted for defeat. For mutual benefit, Zionists are joining in to bring the task to a speedy conclusion. Unfortunately, their strategy is flawed from the start. In abandoning the war in Afghanistan when they had the upper hand to hurriedly declaring war on Iraq, the Zionists and the Christian Zionists have lost on four fronts. First, they lost the initiative of pursuing the remnant of Al-Qaeda in Afghanistan and Pakistan. Second, in widening the war on terror under false pretences they gave an opportunity for the local jihadists and other jihadists around the Islamic world to join the fight and made Iraq, Pakistan, Yemen, Somalia, Algeria, Indonesia their training venues. Third, many moderate Muslims saw the war in Iraq as a war on Islam, which encouraged them to become the subjects for recruitment by Al-Qaeda and other Islamic Jihad organisations. This was happening at a time when America was giving Israel the green light to destroy the Palestinians' dream of their own state. And fourth, America's action in the Middle East is interpreted by moderate Muslims as a new crusades/religious expansionist nationalism through which Christian enemies once again invade Muslim lands.

Above all, moderate Muslims are losing their influence over and control of the extremist elements within their ranks in the same way American and Israeli moderates are losing their control over their own fanatics, the Christian Zionists and the extremist Jewish Zionists. The extremist minorities from all sides now have the momentum to create a euphoric atmosphere for their ideologies to rapidly to get out of control and become a major threat to world peace.

The war in Iraq was seen as the beginning of the new crusade because it was religiously motivated, driven by the aforementioned zealots and spearheaded by George W. Bush and Tony Blair, both considered Christian Zionists with their belief in supporting Israel's expansionist policies as a biblical imperative. They entangled their countries deeper into Middle East politics by deceiving their nations and the rest of the world.

The question to be asked: Why the moderate people, especially the middle class in the Western world, are turning a blind eye to the danger facing their security and the security of future generations from the evil alliance between the far-right Christian Zionists and the extremist Jewish religious nationalists?

In his book *Fiasco: The American Military Adventure in Iraq,* the *Washington Post* military correspondent Thomas E. Ricks wrote: "The Bush administration deceived the American public about the existence of Iraqi weapons of mass destruction that the administration claimed could one day be used against America; weapons that an exhaustive post-invasion search failed to turn up. It already is abundantly apparent in mid-2006 that the US government went to war on Iraq with scant solid international support and on the basis of incorrect information—about weapons of mass destruction and a supposed nexus between Saddam Hussein and Al-Qaeda's terrorism—and then occupied the country negligently."

Ricks points the finger at Donald Rumsfeld and the religious nationalist Zionists Paul Wolfowitz and Douglas Feith for concocting a war plan that resulted in heavy-handed tactics, brutalisation, ineptitude generally, and the killing of many Iraqis that risked driving the country into a civil war. Feith, who served under Wolfowitz before the Iraq war, had a chequered past of covert dealing on behalf of Israel. He was removed from his position as a Middle East analyst at the National Security Council in 1982 when he came under suspicion by the FBI of passing classified material to Israeli embassy officials. Wolfowitz was investigated in 1978 for providing a classified document to an Israeli official on the proposed sale of a US weapons system to an Arab government via AIPAC, the Israel lobby groups.

In 2004, James Petras stated that Bush, Cheney, and Rumsfeld were well aware of the commitment and the agenda of the zealous and influential extremist Jewish nationalist groups working under Paul Wolfowitz in the Pentagon. The group were advocating a sequence of wars against any Muslim regime hostile to Israel and its colonial policy in Palestine. The administration was fully aware of the agenda of these religious nationalists for the simple reason that federal agencies perform exhaustive security clearance checks on all recruits to national security-sensitive areas of the government prior to their employment.

It is unfortunate that the extremism of some Zionists and the Christian Zionists is fuelling Islamic radicalism. The cause of most conflicts is a combination of indoctrination and conditioning by religious and political leaders in their quest for power. The ignorance and insecurity of an average person or a group that constitutes the power base of these leaders is at the heart of the problem. The gullible following of dubious leaders who use religion and nationalism as motivation to designate enemies is the main ingredient for the current clash of civilisations. Throughout history, the clash of civilisations was the main cause behind the rise and the fall of empires. Religion, nationalism, and economic expansion are behind past and current empires. The war on Islam will eventually lead to the demise of the American Empire, as the stage is now set for the opponents' mutual destruction. However, if the moderate majorities from all sides wake up in time, shed their apathy, and take control, they can prevent a major catastrophe. All that is needed for peace and harmony is the entrenchment of secularism or at least the benign interpretation of the so-called heavenly books; or for the enlightened citizens of the world to totally reject religious nationalism. Religious nationalism only leads to vendettas, hatred, and warfare. **Please wake up!**

Religion, Money, and Sex

Removing religion from local and international politics is the best way for the inclusion of all members of society. It is not atheism that is stirring up trouble between churches, synagogues, and mosques. These organisations have a pool of people who are prepared to fight between themselves and with others with the objective of getting as many people as possible into their establishments and to get as much as possible in donations from the rich and powerful. It has nothing to do with religion; it is all about money and power.

Furthermore, these religious organisations are supported by taxpayers' money and by non-secular or semi-secular governments. The money they earn is tax-exempt and their schools are subsidised for a negative outcome of deeper entrenchment of religion in society that leads to more subjectivity, fragmentation, and conflicts.

Alerting the public on how their money is wasted on organisations that give negative social outcome and cause conflict is the duty of every enlightened and objective citizen. Also alerting the public on how these organisations keep re-inventing themselves to maintain the viability of their business, how they put their spin and interpretation on the so-called heavenly books, how they use the fear of God as a major recruiting tool of the ignorant, how they promote the love of God as a romantic tool of the hopeless, and how they use saints to create big business by cashing in on their names and their invention of the afterlife and concepts of heaven and hell are all a ploy to control naïve people. Their ultimate success, however, is their achievement of tax-free status and government subsidies which give them their ultimate social and political power.

Their objective is for individuals to believe in fairy tales instead of themselves.

Fortunately, in future, when self-belief becomes the dominant belief, the religious business will come to an end. Many people now believe that the so-called holy books are written in eras for those same eras and are not applicable to modern times. These books are written for the purposes of war and peace—to live by the sword and die by the sword. They didn't have weapons of mass destruction then and they didn't have a single superpower to act as an international policeman. Above all, the holy books are subject to many interpretations, which because of the fragmentation this engenders, prompts enlightened people to abandon them; in the process, religions become meaningless.

The signs of weakened religion are now evident and proportional to the level of education, technological advances, and the continuous exposure of religious leaders' hypocrisy and their sexual abuse of children. The hypocrisy of practicing what is contrary to what they preach and their sexual abuse of children is well documented and highlighted by their constant apologies and compensation payout to their victims.

To minimise the chances of paedophilia, it is absolutely essential to have zero tolerance against sexual abuse of children. It is useless to listen to repeated apologies from religious leaders for paedophilia in their organisations (especially in the Catholic Church) without abandoning their dogma and taking drastic action against the offenders. Complacent religious leaders who allowed offenders to perpetrate their crimes should be investigated and charged with crimes against humanity.

In the meantime, it is the parents who should feel guilty for exposing their children to paedophilia by sending them to religious schools or by encouraging them to become choir boys in churches run by a historically well known organisation in which where the practice of paedophilia is common. It is the parents' responsibility not to bury their heads in the sand through their blind trust and religious belief. Despite the wide publicity surrounding the matter, some people might say that parents didn't know what was going on. Well, by now they should know and their swift action to protect their children is overdue.

Parents who send their children to these religious places where paedophilia is common should know that leaders of these religious organisations have always covered up and avoided the legal penalties. And it is time for society to deny organised religion their immunity from criminal law. It is time for parents to stop kidding themselves into believing that men of the cloth are innocent and pure, even if they are sexually deprived. It is time for parents to boycott these religious establishments to send a clear message that compels them to change their attitude. It is the only way to make them take notice and change their policy when they know that their attitude is no longer tolerated and their business is under threat.

The evidence from America and Europe points to the fact that no child is safe from sexual abuse by priests, bishops, and cardinals. The core of the problem is sexual desire, which cannot be fulfilled by religious dogma. If the head of these organisations moves to punish all sex predators, there will be not many priests left in the church and not many young men would be willing to be recruited. This will never happen because it would bring the business to an end.

How much evidence do parents need to revolt against the charade of the pope's endless apologies when:

- Pope Benedict XVI himself in 1985, in his capacity as head of the Congregation for the Doctrine of the Faith, signed a letter arguing that the good of the universal church should be considered before the defrocking of an American priest who committed sex offences against two boys
- The cover-up over the sexual abuse of 200 deaf boys in the United States
- The new law in Poland forcing rapists and paedophiles to undergo chemical castration. The procedure, which controls the offender's sex drive, would apply in cases involving sex crimes against children or in cases of incest. Anyone guilty of raping a child under the age of fifteen can now be forced to submit to chemical and psychological therapy to reduce their sex drive at the end of a prison term
- Chemical castration has been tried in France and Canada, but normally on a voluntary basis. The use of compulsory irreversible chemical castration remains the subject of debate in Europe

- A Belgian commission released a report showing harrowing testimony from around 500 cases of alleged sex abuse involving more than 100 victims, thirteen of whom were driven to suicide. The testimony from victims of clergy and church workers reveals another six attempted suicides. The victims were aged between four and twelve. No congregation escaped the Belgian sex abuse and almost every institution, every school, particularly boarding schools, at one time harboured abuse. Two-thirds of the victims were male. In one case, the bishop of Bruges admitted sexually abusing his nephew between 1973 and 1986

- Ireland's Ryan Commission to inquire into child abuse has lasted ten years and its finding, published in early 2009, was followed by the Murphy Commission into sexual abuse of children in the Catholic archdiocese of Dublin (published in November 2009). Both inquiries reported on the shocking conditions under which 35,000 children were held in institutions, many of them from infancy to adulthood. What makes the 2,600-page document so disturbing is that it clearly states that both the church hierarchy and the Irish government knew what was going on but failed to stop the beatings, the rapes, and the humiliation. It shows time and time again that bishops decided that the rape of a child was less significant than the ego, money, and power of their institution. It was part of the system to cover up for rogue elements to protect the reputation of the church. It was a conspiracy and a common practice to move offending priests to other parishes and even out of the country when a compliant was received. The report detailed the crimes and disclosed how the church leaders in Dublin spent decades protecting their paedophile priests from the law. (With tongue in cheek, it could be said that for their penance, offending priests were asked to pray for their victims and say the Hail Mary ten times, or perhaps just three times). The WikiLeaks documents published in December 2010 revealed that requests for information from the 2009 Murphy Commission into sexual and physical abuse by clergy have offended many in the Vatican who felt that the Irish government had "failed to respect and protect Vatican sovereignty during the investigations." The Vatican refused to allow its officials to testify before the Murphy Commission and was angered when they were summoned from Rome. The leaked documents also revealed how the Irish government was forced to grant Vatican officials immunity from testifying to the Murphy Commission

- In America to date, the church has paid over $2.5 billion in compensation to victims of sexual abuse, with more to be paid. This is only in cases that are out in the open; it is estimated that a maximum of 10 percent of people actually come forward to seek closure and to pursue justice and accountability
- The Bishop of Maitland-Newcastle in Australia in 2010 has asked the Pope for help. More than

seventy boys have been abused in his area since the 1970s. Over the past two years, three priests and a clergy member have been charged. One of them was charged with abusing dozens of boys
- The banishment of Mary MacKillop from the church in 1871 for five months after uncovering child sex abuse. Mary MacKillop, the Australian nun who was canonised in 2010, was excommunicated by the church because she discovered children were being abused by a priest and revealed it to the public. In 2009, 100 years after her death, the church publicly apologised for her wrongful excommunication. The story shows that sexual abuse of children has a long history, which will continue until parents decide to boycott and bankrupt the church
- It is worth mentioning that in 2010, Pope Benedict XVI has admitted to the world and to some fifty cardinals that he leads a "wounded and sinner church" as he marked five tumultuous years in charge of a church that is mired in priests' paedophilia scandals. Parents, please wake up!

It is worth commenting on Mary Mackillop (1842–1909) being the latest saint of five who were canonised on October 17, 2010. She has been beatified earlier for one miracle, the cure of a woman from terminal leukemia in 1961, which was many decades after Mary Mackillop's death. She needed a second miracle to become a saint. She achieved sainthood by the confirmation of her second miracle in early 2010 on the basis of another woman's claim of having been cured of inoperable cancer by *praying to*

Mary MacKillop. Her canonisation was a result of lobbying by the Australian government and Sister Maria Casey, a former sister of Saint Joseph, which shows that lobbying and bargaining (and possibly time travel) are essential elements in becoming a saint. To divert attention from recent worldwide negative publicity against the church for its cover-ups of child sex abuse by its priests, the hierarchy was able to mobilise all resources to promote the canonisation of Mary MacKillop.

To further divert attention from recent bad publicity, in January 2011 Pope Benedict XVI started a new circus with the beatification of Pope John Paul II for the miraculous cure of a French nun who suffered from Parkinson's disease. The May 1 ceremony is expected to draw hundreds of thousands of pilgrims to Rome to celebrate the first miracle of the pope. A second miracle is needed for John Paul to be made a saint. **It is guaranteed.**

The unintended consequence of the circus, unfortunately, is the brainwashing of many new young brains, which are swept up in the stage-managed euphoria that will keep the religious business going until the next major scandal … which will be followed by the discovery of yet undiscovered saints.

The strange aspect of the canonisation of Mary MacKillop is the church allowing women to become saints, but not allowing them to become priests. It is ironic that Mary MacKillop was canonised when earlier the church considered her disobedient by virtue of defying church authority. Accordingly, the church has in effect canonised a disobedient saint, which makes its credibility and infallibility questionable.

How can educated people still seriously think that God is a reasonable explanation for anything? How can a modern secular society explain some events as the work of an invisible man in the sky? The celebration of Mary MacKillop's miracle cancer cures is a worrying example for its lack of scientific backing. The question is not whether somebody has recovered from cancer after praying to MacKillop but how many others prayed and did *not* get cured?

Faith is a personal thing and if some people want to believe, then there is nothing on earth that will prevent them from doing so. People are more likely to take notice and amplify in their minds everything that may support their dogmatic beliefs. Dogmatic beliefs usually lead to superstition, which in turn leads to irrational thinking. Is it rational, for example, for some people to claim that they won the lotto by praying to God or to the devil? Hope and the power of positive thinking are in play here, not prayer. Putting too much emphasis on faith could have negative impact on patients if they come to the conclusion that their sickness is a divine punishment for their sins, which make them abandon positive thinking and surrender to the will of God. Is belief in fairy tales a legitimate substitute for proven medicine, optimism, self-confidence, and self-belief?

Enlightened people with cancer do not prefer to pray for a future saints for a cure many years before they are considered for sainthood. A devoted Christian usually prays directly to God because it is contrary to Christian faith to pray for anyone else except Jesus. Perhaps, addiction to faith with its illusional and delusional action has the placebo effect. The ultimate beneficiary from addiction to faith is the religious organisations. The blind faith brings with it the proceeds from pilgrimage, donations, statues, and other souvenirs sales that will end up in the church coffers, making it richer and more powerful.

Finally, why does God give cancer to so many good people and allow Mary MacKillop to cure only two—while the others die in agony? **Who are they kidding?**

Religion is a poison: In his book *God is Not Great: How Religion Poison Everything*, the English-American author and journalist Christopher Hitchens says religion poisons everything. Religion attacks people in their deepest integrity by saying that nobody can make a moral decision without it and that a supernatural dictatorship is the only hope. It is also hard to refute his argument against religious claim that faith offers comfort. He writes, "How can religions offer comfort when for many centuries they were causing conflicts and wars that have resulted in massive destruction and countless casualties? Just by reading the major religious texts, it is easy to see how religions provoke atrocities and discrimination. Judging from the history of religion, when the conditions are right, it can take control and become totalitarian and corrupting." Hitchens also points out that religion was invented by man when humans were illiterate, but now, an ethical life can be lived without it and religion can be replaced with reasoning and an open mind in pursuit of ideas and facts.

Religious leaders promote the idea that morality is God-given and their followers think that without religion nobody would know right from wrong. This is a gross misrepresentation of reality when a majority of non-believers' moral standards can surpass the moral standards of any believer, including religious leaders. Additionally, a harmonious and stable society can only begin when a secular system is established and later entrenched. In actual fact, the commercialisation of religion has resulted in the loss of its meaning. Fundamentalists of various religions are using faith to justify the cruelty and calamity mankind has experienced since the invention of God and the birth of the first religion.

What morality can religions be proud of when they discriminate against half of the world's population—women. The Vatican's recent revisions that put the ordination of women on par with child sex abuse drew howls of protest from around the world. This is what the church is all about; it has openly and actively discriminated against women since its inception. It can also be seen from the orthodox Jewish prayer in which men thank God for not making them women (meaning in this context that religion is meant only for men). Another brutal aspect of religious discrimination against women is seen in Islam. It is estimated that 5,000 Muslim women and girls are shot, strangled, stoned, and burned by their own families every year in an effort to restore "the family honour." In all the major religions' holy books there are countless examples to demonstrate that the foundations of the patriarchal religions are built on an inherent message that women are inferior to men. Even the debate about women's status and role in religion is dominated by men. This is when women often lose, despite the fact that religious leaders always target women as an essential part of their power base because women are more easily attracted to religious moral messages than men. **Women of the world, please wake up!**

Final Word

It is never too late

Capitalism is a good thing, but when it crosses over to the dark side it is no longer a good thing; it becomes extremely dangerous. Work hard, make some money, and spend that money on luxuries if you will, but do not spend it on a hidden agenda of control of a nation or its people. Unfortunately, the adoption by America of extreme capitalism and economic expansionist policies is driving it into aggression, especially since it became the world's only superpower after winning the Cold War. Its aggression is also encouraged greatly by Israel lobby groups who are behind Israel's territorial expansionist policies in Palestine. Aggressive colonial expansion requires huge financial support and manpower capacity to counter the huge resentment and resistance it generates. America and Israel don't understand that influence, not power, is ultimately the most valuable strategy. Influence comes from magnanimity and reaps greater gains. The use of power results in resentment and reaction, which ultimately weakens and destroys the aggressor.

The use of power in Iraq, Pakistan, and Afghanistan, where America has heavily relied on its air force instead of the use of its army, didn't take into account the extent of revolt and resistance it would generate. It didn't take into account the need to protect the civilian population, which has resulted in great loss of life that has made America the most hated country in the world. Its brutal approach is causing many casualties and devastation of other nations' infrastructure. In the name of fighting terrorism (while hiding their ambition of economic expansion and the control of world energy resources) America is engaged in the slaughter of many innocent people.

America, with its glory now reduced to a declining power that has succumbed to the whim of fanatical Israeli settlers who have awesome power over Israel's policies and, indirectly, over America's foreign policies, which is directly provoking Islamic terrorism. The destructive activities of Israeli settlers are capable of producing a "black swan" event. These are events that are totally unexpected and have a disproportionately high impact on society. Examples include the September 11 attacks and the start of World War I. Future black swan events might include a terrorist attack with nuclear and/or biological weapons.

However, should America decide that enough is enough and move to stop the destructive activities of the settlers and the Israeli onslaught on the Palestinians, a calamity can be averted. America is the only country in a position to stop the calamity by curtailing the power of the extremist pro-Israel lobby groups in America, who are in control of its foreign policies and its Congress. In defiance of Israel lobby groups, America can easily vote yes in the UN Security Council for the establishment of a viable Palestinian state with 1967 borders. This is the first step towards curbing Israeli aggression in the region, especially against its Arab neighbours.

Failing that, America's and Israel's interests around the world will be a constant target of Muslim extremists, and with no end in sight. Solving the Palestinian problem and controlling Israel's aggression would empower all moderate Muslims to turn against the extremist elements within, instead of the moderates becoming a source for recruitment by the extremists. As it stands, the terror network is evolving to become more creative, more flexible, and more agile, with a capacity to acquire weapons of mass destruction.

America, in the meantime, is losing the world's trust and many of its allies are now questioning the wisdom of the alliance and their assumption of relying on America for ensuring their security. America as a superpower is in a position to set the security agenda for its allies, but with its decline its task now is beyond reach, especially while it is fighting for its own survival. America's woes are self-inflicted by its one-sided expansionist ambitions to control the world and its resources using all possible means, including religious war. Adding to America's woes is the decline in its future productivity as a result of its huge debt. Securing future economic growth to pay off its debts can only be achieved by additional spending on education, health, and infrastructure and by spending less on wars. Unfortunately the conflicting agendas of the Republicans and the Democrats will prevent this from happening. The Republicans want to fight wars till death, whilst the Democrats want to prolong America's life by exiting wars.

America has a choice, to continue with its costly wars and self-destruction or to create a peaceful world that is built on a win-win principle instead of its current winner-takes-all principle. The first can be achieved by adopting a moderate capitalism that embodies the fair distribution of wealth and rejecting extreme capitalism that leads to the rich getting richer and the poor getting poorer. The culture and psychology of moderate capitalism will lead to give–and-take as a better guiding principle to human and international relations. The starting point for America to become a reasonable country is by its developing exit strategies to end the unnecessary wars against Islamic countries: First, it needs to remove the majority of its military bases from around the world, especially the ones that provoking resentment and insurgency, which are set up to attack other nations rather than defend America. Second, act decisively to establish a viable Palestinian state. Third, it needs to clean up the CIA, which is acting inhumanely and is out of control and acting as a government within a government.

America has a choice: to stay the course as an expansionist empire or to become a great empire. To be a great empire is to allow poorer countries to prosper and for more people to become consumers instead of refugees or enemies of the empire.

America's wars in Iraq and Afghanistan and its helping Israel with its war on the Palestinians are leading to an inevitable clash between the Zionists and Christian Zionists on the one hand and the Islamic world on the other. If wisdom is allowed to prevail, this clash can be averted before the Palestinians and the rest of the Islamic world decide to adopt the motto of "don't get mad, get even." To prevent mutually assured destruction, aggression and the desire for domination and control must be abandoned.

Above all, America and Israel must understand that spreading fear through their military power can have two consequences: First, fear can destroy people. Second, fear can drive people by triggering their survival instinct to fight.

It is necessary to understand that revolutions and religions came about as a consequence of resentment and resistance engendered by the injustices inflicted on people. "Live and let live" instead of "live and let die" is the best solution to many human conflicts. The application of true justice for everyone is a prerequisite for peace and harmony in the world.

The Jews' suffering during World War II should be a lesson that no nation should suffer the consequences of fascism. Israel's policy of segregation, ethnic cleansing, and the construction of the apartheid wall are no different from what happened in South Africa. In the process of the implementation of the Zionist project, Israel has tried to destroy the Palestinian nation, and this is causing a huge Islamic backlash. Israel is acting with impunity, supported by imperialist America on the grounds of self-defence, when in fact it is the provocateur, the aggressor, and the occupier of Palestinian land. The self-defence argument is a powerful piece of propaganda, one that America has become comfortable in hiding behind while maintaining its blind, unfair, and unconditional commitment to Israel.

Wisdom and moderation can make Israel the most prosperous country in the world, if it abandons its religious nationalism and embraces a reasonable two-state solution, which would make it an acceptable neighbour with access to huge markets throughout the Arab and Islamic worlds. Israel's current behaviour is based on the instinct of survival but ignores the fact that civilisation and human evolution have advanced far beyond the law of the jungle. Its leadership's behaviour is not in tune with its sophisticated and highly educated population. Israel's arrogant settlements expansion into Palestinians land is in violation of international laws and in contradiction of the peace process, with which it pretends to be engaged, although a negotiated agreement revolves around the total evacuation of Jewish settlements from Palestinian territories to 1967 borders.

Israel's utilisation of America's military strength to destroy a helpless nation contradicts all human rights principles. By enlisting America's backing to sideline international laws and by expanding Jewish settlements in the occupied territories, Israel is seriously miscalculating the final outcome, especially by not taking into consideration the rapid decline of America. America's rapid decline relates to its lack of understanding that the radical Islamic terrorism towards it is fuelled by its failure to resolve the Israeli-Palestinian conflict and its lack of understanding that poverty, unemployment, injustice, and ignorance are the main driver of terrorism.

Christian Zionists, Jewish extremist Zionists, Muslim fundamentalists, and all other fundamentalists around the world have to understand that money, nationalism and religion are the evil weapons that are fragmenting the world and that a fragmented world is a threat to their own survival and the survival of human race.

Despite the fact that fragmentation of the world is a human compulsion—especially in economics, nationalism, and religion—the human race can still avoid its self-destruction by activating the instinct of the survival of the species. The greater need to preserve human life requires the examination of how individuals, groups and nations are contributing to the fragmentation of the world, especially in their following of sinister, extremist, and divisive political and religious leaders. To secure the future of the world, it is essential to curb extremism on all sides before it is too late; and it is the duty of all moderate people around the globe to act now, as they are the people best-equipped to control the extremists within.

Finally, a wise lesson can be learnt from the physicist David Bohm (a protégé of Albert Einstein), who said: **"Our current way of fragmenting the world into parts, not only doesn't work, but may even lead to our extinction."**

Please wake up before it is too late!

Sources

Encyclopaedia Britannica

Encyclopaedia Microsoft Encarta

Wikipedia

The Bible

Kenneth J. Hagan and Ian J. Bickerton, *Unintended Consequences: The United States at War*. London: Reaktion Books, 2007.

Niall Ferguson, *The Ascent of Money: The Financial History of the World*. New York: Penguin Books, 2009.

Paul Kennedy, *Rise and Fall of the Great Powers*. New York: Random House, 1987.

Hani Montan, *Thorny Opinion*. Charleston-USA: BookSurge, 2008.

James Petras, *The Power of Israel in the United States*. Atlanta-USA: Clarity Press, 2006.

Saul P.Cortez, *Israel No Longer Chosen*. Charleston-USA: BookSurge, 2007.

John J. Mearsheimer and Stephen M. Walt, *The Israel Lobby and U.S. Foreign policy*. New York: Farrar, Straus and Giroux, 2008.

Paul Findley, *They Dare to Speak Out: People and Institutions Confront Israel's Lobby*. Chicago: Lawrence Hill Books, 2003.

Ian J. Bickerton, *The Arab-Israeli Conflict*. London: Reaktion Books, 2009.

Lawrence G. McDonald and Patrick Robinson, *A Colossal Failure of Common Sense: The inside Story of the Collapse of Lehman Brothers*. New York: Crown Publishing Group, 2009.

Gary Rivlin, *Broke, USA*. New York: Harper Collins, 2010.

George Friedman, *America's Secret War: Inside the Hidden Worldwide Struggle Between the United States and Its Enemies*. New York: Broadway Books, 2004.

Z magazine June 1999; "A Brief History of U.S. Interventions: 1945 to the Present" Article by William Blum.

James Mills, *The Underground Empire: Where Crime and Governments Embrace*. New York: Dell Books, 1987.

Christopher Robbins, *Air America*. New York: Avon Books, 1985.

Alfred W. McCoy, *The Politics of Heroin in Southeast Asia: The CIA Complicity in the Global Drug Trade*. Chicago: Lawrence Hill Books, 2003.

John Dinges, *Our Man in Panama*. New York: Three Rivers Press, 1991.

Jonathan Kwitny, *The Crime of Patriots: A True Tale of Dope, Dirty Money and the CIA*. Florida-USA: Touchstone Books, 1988.

Steve Coll, *Ghost Wars: The Secret History of the CIA, Afghanistan, and Bin Laden, from the Soviet Invasion to September 10, 2001*. New York: Penguin, 2004.

Grant F. Smith and Michael Scheuer, *Spy Trade: How Israel's Lobby Undermine America's Economy*. Washington: Institute for Research of Middle Eastern Policy, 2009.

Sasha Polakow-Suransky, *The Unspoken Alliance: Israel's Secret Alliance with Apartheid South Africa*. New York: Pantheon Books, 2010.

Michael Scheuer, *Imperial Hubris: Why the West is Losing the War on Terror*. Dulles-USA: Potomac Books, 2007.

Washington Post newspaper July 19, 2010; "Top Secret America" report by Dana Priest and William Arkin.

Alfred W. McCoy, A *Question of Torture: CIA Interrogation, from the Cold War to the War on Terror (American Empire Project)*. New York: Holt Paperbacks, 2006.

Chomsky. Info, May 24, 2009; "The Torture Memos" by Noam Chomsky.

The Independent newspaper October 24, 2010; "The Shaming of America" article by Robert Fisk.

Robert Baer, *See No Evil: The True Story of a Ground Soldier in the CIA's War on Terrorism*. New York: Broadway, 2003.

Robert Baer, *Blow The House Down: A Novel*. New York: Crown Publishing Group, 2006.

Belfer Centre for Science and International Affairs April 13, 2010; "Securing the Bomb" report by Harvard Kennedy School and Nuclear Threat Initiative, Harvard University.

Bob Woodward, *Obama's War*. New York: Simon & Schuster, 2010.

Thomas Ricks, *The Gamble: General Petraes and the American Adventure in Iraq*. New York: Penguin Books, 2010.

Richard A. Clarke, *Against All Enemies: Inside America's War on Terror*. New York: Free Press, 2004.

Bob Drogin, *Curveball: Spies, Lies, and the Con Man Who Caused a War*. New York: Random House, 2007.

James Bamford, *A Pretext for War: 9/11, Iraq, and the Abuse of America's Intelligence Agencies*. New York: Anchor Books, 2005.

Jimmy Carter, *Palestine: Peace Not Apartheid*. New York: Simon & Schuster, 2007.

Peace and Justice Post July 30, 2007; "Guillotining Gaza" article by Noam Chomsky.

Chomsky. Info, June 6, 2009; "Exterminate all the Brutes: Gaza 2009" article of by Noam Chomsky.

Sydney Morning Herald January 8, 2009; "Shocking cynicism of a poisoned homeland" article by novelist Sara Dowse.

United Nations Fact Finding Mission on the Gaza Conflict September 29, 2009; report from the Hon. Judge Richard Goldstone commission of inquiry.

Norman G. Finkelstein, *The Holocaust Industry: Reflection on the Exploitation of Jewish Suffering*. New York: Verso Books, 2003.

Norman G. Finkelstein, *Beyond the Chutzpah: On the Misuse of Anti-Semitism and the Abuse of History*. Berkeley: California University Press, 2008.

Victor Ostrovsky, *By Way of Deception: The Making of Mossad officer*. London: Wilshire Press, 2002.

Edward S. Herman and Noam Chomsky, *Manufacturing Consent: The Political Economy of the Mass Media*. New York: Pantheon Books, 2002.

Noam Chomsky, *Media Control: The Spectacular Achievements of Propaganda*. New York: Open Media, 2003.

Ilan Pappe, *The Ethnic Cleansing of Palestine*. Oxford: Oneworld Publications, 2007.

Ilan Pappe, *A History of Modern Palestine: One Land, Two People*. Cambridge: Cambridge University Press, 2006.

Alan Hart, *Zionism is the Real Enemy of the Jews*. Atlanta-USA: Clarity Press, 2009.

Rosemary Radford and Herman Ruether, *The Wrath of Jonah: The Crisis of Religious Nationalism in the Israeli-Palestinian Conflict*. Philadelphia: Fortress Press, 2002.

Jacqueline Rose, *The Question of Zion*. New Jersey: Princeton University Press, 2007.

Thomas E. Ricks, *Fiasco: The American Military Adventure in Iraq*. Westminster-UK: Penguin Press, 2006.

Christopher Hitchens, *God is Not Great: How Religion Poison Everything*. New York: Hachette Books, 2009.

www.ingramcontent.com/pod-product-compliance
Lightning Source LLC
Chambersburg PA
CBHW030252290526
45785CB00001B/63